Understanding
⸺ THE ⸺
SOCIOPATH

Understanding
⏤⏤•⊢THE⊣•⏤⏤
SOCIOPATH

Why antisocials, narcissists and psychopaths break the rules of life

DONNA ANDERSEN

Anderly Publishing
Egg Harbor Township, New Jersey

Back cover photography by Bill Horin

Anderly Publishing
3121-D Fire Road, #304
Egg Harbor Township, NJ 08234 USA
www.anderlypublishing.com

Library of Congress Control Number: 2019948924
ISBN: 978-1-951347-01-7

First softcover edition October 2019

Contents

Introduction

I married a con man. James Alwyn Montgomery, my ex-husband, took $227,000 from me. He cheated with at least six different women during our two-and-a-half-year involvement. He had a child with one of those women, and then, 10 days after I left him, he married the mother of the child. It was the second time he committed bigamy.

I certainly didn't know all of this was going to happen when I met him. Montgomery swept me off my feet and showered me with affection. He told me I was the woman he'd been waiting for all his life. Together, he promised, we'd make his entrepreneurial dreams come true, and we'd soon be living in the lap of luxury.

When everything fell apart, and I discovered the extent of his lies and deception, my head was spinning. I simply could not understand his behavior. I asked my therapist, "What kind of person does this?"

"He sounds like a sociopath," she said.

A sociopath? What was that?

Like most of us, I'd heard the word, but didn't really understand what it meant. So I started researching. The first book I read was, *Without Conscience — The disturbing world of the psychopaths around us,* by Robert Hare, Ph.D. The people Hare described sounded much like my ex — except for the fact that most of them were convicted criminals. James Montgomery, as far as I knew, had never spent time in prison.

Most of the research on people who have exploitative personality disorders — antisocial, narcissistic, borderline, histrionic or psychopathic — is done on two groups of people: prisoners and college students. Why? Because those are the populations that researchers can access.

People who have antisocial, narcissistic or psychopathic personality disorders rarely seek therapy, so psychology researchers have few opportunities to gather clinical data on them. As a result, little information is available on how people with these disorders behave "in the community," which means outside of prison or mental institutions.

Because of my experience, I launched Lovefraud.com in 2005. Since then, I've been able to gather information from thousands of people who came to believe that their romantic partners, family members, friends or acquaintances were disordered. More than 10,000 people have shared their stories or completed Lovefraud's online surveys.

On Lovefraud.com, I refer to these disordered individuals collectively as "sociopaths." When psychologist George E. Partridge coined the term in 1930, he suggested using it to describe, "anything deviated or pathological in social relations." He wanted "sociopathy" to describe a pathological condition in which people are maladjusted in their relations with others and society, and motivated towards antisocial behavior. This is how I use the word on Lovefraud — "sociopathy" is an umbrella term that encompasses the multiple official diagnoses of antisocial, narcissistic, borderline and histrionic personality disorders, and psychopathy.

Best of the Lovefraud Blog Series

Lovefraud.com now offers thousands of articles. It's great information, but because it's spread out over years of blog archives, the information is not always easy to find. To make it more accessible, I've collected, organized and updated the articles into this Best of the Lovefraud Blog series of books:

- *Understanding the Sociopath*
- *Seduced by a Sociopath*
- *Dealing with Sociopaths*
- *Recovery from a Sociopath*

Understanding the Sociopath explains the millions of exploiters who live among us, blending easily in our society. You'll learn that yes, they truly do exist. You'll learn how they typically behave. My hope is that with this information, you can spot them and get them out of your life — before too much damage is done.

10 facts to help you explain
your experience with a sociopath

The biggest reason why we get tangled up with sociopaths is that we don't know they exist. We don't know they live among us, so we don't watch out for them, so we get in trouble.

Then, when we try to tell our friends and families what happened, they have no idea what we're talking about — because they don't know sociopaths exist either. So on top of the devastation we endure from the sociopath, when we turn to others for support, we are not understood or even believed.

If you're trying to explain your experience with a sociopath, here are some facts to help you put your story in context:

1. Approximately 30 million people in the United States — 12% of women and 16% of men — could be diagnosed with exploitative personality disorders. The specific diagnoses are antisocial, narcissistic, borderline or histrionic personality disorder, or psychopathy. (For convenience, Lovefraud refers to them collectively as "sociopaths.")

2. Despite what you see in the media and movies, sociopaths and psychopaths are not all serial killers. Most of them never kill anyone — in fact, many are never even convicted of any crimes.

3. Sociopaths can be found in all demographic groups — male, female, old, young, rich, poor, all nationalities, all races, all professions. They are everywhere.

4. Sociopaths look just like the rest of us — some are handsome, some are homely. They do not look like they're crazy. They easily blend into society.

5. Although most people understand the word "antisocial" to mean someone is a loner with no social skills, people who have antisocial personality disorder are often friendly, charming, gregarious and fun. The mental health field chose bad terminology — no wonder we're all confused.

6. Sociopaths are skilled liars. They are so good at deception and manipulation that anyone can fall for their lies. They can fool cops and psychologists, so the rest of us don't have a chance.

7. Sociopaths do not have the ability to love — this is the core of the disorder. They literally do not feel love the way the rest of us do, in that they will never put the welfare of someone else before their own — not even the welfare of their children. If they do appear concerned about your welfare, it is an act so that they can exploit you later.

8. Sociopaths feel entitled to get what they want, when they want it and how they want it. Sociopaths also have no empathy and no conscience. Taken together, this means they will do absolutely anything to get what they want, and don't care whom they hurt in the process.

9. A key way that sociopaths manipulate others is by trying to make you feel sorry for them. They tell sad stories about their problems and the people who hurt them, all with the objective of convincing you to give them what they want.

10. Antisocials and psychopaths are profoundly different from the rest of us. They love being the puppet master, and are motivated by power and control. But because of the way most of us have grown up, believing that "we're all created equal" and "there's good in everyone," we are susceptible to their deceit and manipulation.

Sociopaths range from sleazy to serial killer

*L*ovefraud received the following email from a reader whom we'll call "Jason."

> My best friend of 20 years I believe is a sociopath. It's very sad because you want to give a person the benefit of the doubt, but after awhile it becomes apparent. He displays all the characteristics of the sociopath. I'm smart, but I can't convince myself with 100% certainty that he's a sociopath (maybe most people can't.) It's hard to reconcile with it. Is there any advice you can give me?

Yes, Jason. First I'll give the somewhat easy explanation; then I'll give the more technical explanation.

Cluster of traits and behaviors

The first thing to understand is that sociopaths are not all the same. This disorder encompasses a cluster of traits and behaviors. Any particular individual can have any of the traits and behaviors to greater or lesser degrees. Therefore, some sociopaths are definitely worse than others. They can range from sleazy to serial killer.

In fact, it's often the low- to mid-level sociopaths who are most difficult to identify. Maybe they aren't as grandiose as others. Maybe they sometimes seem to have empathy. Maybe they aren't always aggressive. So they seem to have many of the negative traits, but not all of them — and you wonder if they really are sociopaths.

Professionals do not agree

Making matters even more complicated, mental health professionals do not agree on what to call these disordered individuals, and how they should be diagnosed. In fact, the word "sociopath" is no longer used as a clinical diagnosis.

Lovefraud, however, has proposed using the word "sociopath" as a general umbrella term to describe people who live their lives by exploiting others. This would include people who are clinically diagnosed as having antisocial, narcissistic, borderline or histrionic personality disorders, or psychopathy.

Psychopathy Checklist Revised

The best way to evaluate someone's degree of psychopathy, one of the disorders, is the Psychopathy Checklist Revised (PCL-R), developed by Dr. Robert Hare. This is a formal evaluation that should only be done by a trained clinician.

The evaluation is based on a set of 20 traits and behaviors. They are:

Antisocial behavior
- Need for stimulation and proneness to boredom
- Parasitic lifestyle
- Poor behavioral control
- Sexual promiscuity
- Lack of realistic long-term goals
- Impulsivity
- Irresponsibility
- Early behavior problems
- Juvenile delinquency
- Parole or probation violations

Emotional/interpersonal traits
- Glibness and superficial charm
- Grandiose sense of self-worth
- Pathological lying
- Conning and manipulativeness
- Lack of remorse or guilt

17

- Shallow affect
- Callousness and lack of empathy
- Failure to accept responsibility for own actions

Other factors
- Committing a wide variety of crimes
- Having many short-term marital relationships

The clinician determines the degree to which an individual exhibits each trait, giving a score of 0, 1, or 2.

- 0 — the trait is not present
- 1 — the trait is somewhat present
- 2 — the trait is a reasonably good match

The maximum score on the PCL-R is 40, meaning the person scored 2 on every item. Someone who scores 40 is really, really disordered. The average person, who is not disordered, scores around 4.

"A psychopath"

Dr. Hare actually says no one should be called "a psychopath." Hare prefers to say, "This person scored (the number) on the PCL-R."

Why? Because although most experts say that anyone who scores 30 or above is "a psychopath," this dividing line is somewhat arbitrary.

What about someone who scores 18? Or 25? This person is far nastier than an average person who scores 4, but is not considered to be "a psychopath."

Another researcher, Dr. Reid Meloy, addressed this issue by clarifying degrees of disturbance. Here's how he rates different PCL-R scores:
- 10-19 — mild psychopathic disturbance
- 20-29 — moderate psychopathic disturbance
- 30-39 — severe psychopathic disturbance

Feeling exploited

As you can see, it is difficult to say precisely if someone is "a psychopath" or "a sociopath." But about the only time that it's important to diagnose someone with precision is during a court trial.

If you are making a decision about whether or not to have any involvement with someone, you don't need to know his or her score on the PCL-R. All you need to consider is if you feel exploited. If you do, then you should put the person out of your life.

The answer:
Why psychopaths do what they do

Perhaps the biggest question asked by people who have been targeted by psychopaths is, "Why?"

1. Why did he work so hard to win me, proclaiming his love and promising a beautiful future together, and then suddenly dump me?
2. Why does she intentionally scare, upset, demean and embarrass her own children?
3. Why does he lie about stupid things, even when he'd be better off telling the truth?
4. Why doesn't she care that she's hurting me?

I'm sure you have your own list of "why?" questions.

We try to make sense of the psychopath's unfathomable behavior. We look for explanations that we can understand: Perhaps he was abused or felt abandoned as a child. Perhaps she has low self-esteem. Perhaps he's under a lot of stress at work.

There must be a reason, we tell ourselves, because normal people just don't act that way.

Here's what you need to understand: Psychopaths are NOT NORMAL.

Please don't respond with, "Well, duh."

The degree to which these people are NOT NORMAL is truly astounding, and difficult to absorb. But it's key to understanding the "why."

Terminology

First, some explanation of terminology. Generally, when I write articles on Lovefraud, I refer to the disordered people we discuss here as "sociopaths." I use that word as an umbrella term encompassing all people with personality disorders who live their lives by exploiting others. It covers several clinical diagnoses — psychopathy and antisocial, narcissistic, borderline and histrionic personality disorders.

Usually I don't bother differentiating among the various disorders. The conditions overlap, and they're all bad news for anyone who gets snagged by these exploiters. From the victim's point of view, arguing over the terminology is like splitting hairs. But sometimes there is value in explaining one of the disorders.

Psychopaths cannot love

Psychopaths are NOT NORMAL because they are missing the traits that are essential to our humanity. According to Dr. Liane Leedom, psychopaths have no ability to love. They cannot truly care for another person, or put anyone's interests ahead of their own.

Think about what that means. Think of all the things you've done out of love for another person — your parents, your spouse, your children, your friends, your military buddies.

Now think about what it must be like to be someone for whom the motivation of love simply does not exist.

Psychopaths are like the Terminator characters from the movies. I'm referring to the bad guys — Arnold Schwarzenegger in the first Terminator movie, the shape-shifter in the second movie. They can think, analyze, learn and evaluate. They can mimic human emotion. But they cannot love, and they have no conscience.

Their emptiness is frightening. Just like the emptiness of a psychopath.

Psychopathic motivation

So what motivates a psychopath? Why do they do what they do?

Dr. Lianne Leedom says psychopaths are motivated by three things:

- Power
- Control
- Sex

That's it.

So let's look again at the questions from the beginning of this article, questions that you may have asked yourself:

1. *Why did he work so hard to win me, proclaiming his love and promising a beautiful future together, and then suddenly dump me?* Despite what he said, it was never about love. He liked the power of seducing you, and the sex.

2. *Why does she intentionally scare, upset, demean and embarrass her own children?* She feels no love for them. She only wants to control them.

3. *Why does he lie about stupid things, even when he'd be better off telling the truth?* Lies change what you believe, which is a form of power. Some experts call it "duping delight." Psychopaths like it.

4. *Why doesn't she care that she's hurting me?* She has no ability to care about your emotional pain. But she does like the power of making you feel emotional pain.

Yes, it's really that bad. Psychopaths feel no love. They are driven only by their desires for:

- Power
- Control
- Sex

The eyes of a sociopath

Sociopaths are hiding in all segments of society. They can be male, female, all races, all religions, all ethnic groups, old, young, rich, poor, good-looking, homely. Only one aspect of their appearance may hint at their personality disorder:

The eyes.

If you've had any type of involvement with a sociopath, you may have noticed some weirdness about the person's eyes. You may see this in one or more ways, such as:

Intense eye contact

In my book, *Red Flags of Love Fraud*, one of the 10 warning signs is intense eye contact. To gather information for the book, I conducted the Lovefraud Romantic Partners Survey. Of the 1,352 survey respondents, 59% of them reported that their sociopathic partner engaged in intense eye contact.

Here's how one woman described the moment she met the sociopath:

> It was the most intense eye contact that I have ever experienced. So much so that it was all I could describe years later when I recalled "how we met." His eyes burned into my soul even though they were brown, and I didn't like brown eyes!

The stare

Many Lovefraud readers also mention how the sociopaths stared at them. Here's an email from a man about his ex-wife:

It has been my experience with a sociopath ex-wife that there are different reasons behind the stare. I saw the angry predator stare but I also saw other stares.

Before I started dating my wife I would catch her staring at me in church and I would think that this woman is interested in me, let's go talk to her. She had two sons by two different men; one was eight and the other was four.

The first three weeks were great, then for some unknown reason she started expressing her anger at me. At first it was over small things but eventually grew into full time hatred. I would catch her staring at me at different times and wonder what she was doing. Turns out she was studying me very closely.

I learned in church that everything was either good or evil, moral or immoral. But studying psychology, I found a third category: amoral or non-moral. Money is amoral; it is neither good nor evil, but how people use it shows their heart is good or evil. Emotions are also amoral — they are neither good nor evil, but how you choose to react to them makes you good or evil.

My father, when angry, would raise his voice and yell, so I followed his example as an adult and as a father. I saw, however, that not everyone yelled when angry. Some got very quiet, some would leave and come back later when calmed down.

My ex-wife would provoke me to anger with insults or other unkind words. I chose one day to pick a different reaction when angry. I would blow it off or be quiet. My ex-wife picked up on this right away and said in frustration that I was unpredictable when angry: You used to yell, now you just blow it off. I was floored at how quick she pick up on this change in my behavior and how it frustrated her attempts to provoke me to anger. I thought either she has an IQ in the four-digit range, or she has experience in this area before.

The stare was her studying my emotions and my chosen reactions to my emotions. She could read me like a book, and manipulated me to get her desired reaction out of me. I was amazed. I saw that she did this with everyone and could very easy manipulate others to her will.

Lifeless eyes

This is what I sometimes saw with my ex-husband. When he wasn't actively engaged in manipulating me or someone else, his eyes seemed to indicate that there was nobody home inside.

In two Lovefraud surveys, I asked respondents if they agreed with this statement about their disordered romantic partners: "Sometimes, the individual's eyes seemed to be lifeless." In the Romantic Partner Survey, 60% of respondents agreed. In the Female Sociopath Survey, 57% of respondents agreed.

Because sociopaths can be so charming, exciting and magnetic, it can be difficult to spot this characteristic of lifeless eyes. Sometimes the best place to see it is in a photograph.

Black eyes

I've had many people tell me that when the sociopath was in a rage, his eyes turned totally black. I've only heard this about male sociopaths so far — if anyone has seen this in a female, please let me know.

Here's a letter from a woman who was married to a male sociopath:

> One occurrence to this day puts chills up my spine and tears in my eyes.
>
> The night my husband held me at gunpoint with a loaded hunting rifle, something terrifying happened. My husband's eyes are bright, light blue. He has beautiful eyes, so bright you notice them from across a room.
>
> But that night, when he attacked me, his eyes were black. Not just black but so black it goes beyond words. If you've ever watched the movie Amityville Horror, there's a scene when the father has become deeply possessed and he turns on his family.
>
> MY SPOUSE LOOKED 100% IDENTICAL TO THAT

MAN!

AFTER THE INCIDENT I BEGAN TO QUESTION MY SANITY. BLUE EYES DON'T TURN BLACK. EYES CHANGE COLOR, BUT NO HUMAN HAS EYES LIKE THAT.

I researched it, and lo and behold there have been numerous cases dealing with narcissists and/or sociopaths where blue eyes were noted to have turned black when they were enraged!

How horrifying is that? It's as though there is another being inside these people!

I still have nightmares. Never before nor since has he ever demonstrated that behavior. He says he doesn't remember any of it. (No, I don't think drugs and I know no alcohol was involved.)

Please warn your readers.

Pay attention

If you experience intense eye contact, or see the predatory stare, lifeless eyes, or frightening black eyes, know that these are the only possible physical signs that you are involved with a sociopath.

You may see the scary eyes for only a moment, before the sociopath regains control and starts love bombing or manipulating you. Do not doubt your perception. Do not tell yourself that you are imagining things.

It's said that the eyes are the windows of the soul. If you see eyes that make you doubt there is a soul inside, pay attention. You may have just seen the truth.

5 reasons why the sociopath's behavior in your relationship makes no sense

Shock. Confusion. Disbelief. These are common experiences when you're romantically involved with a sociopath.

You ask yourself, or your friends, or your therapist, questions like:

"How can he be talking about getting married one day and ghost me the next?"

"How can she be so mean and cruel and then act like nothing ever happened?"

"How can he tell me that he loves me while he's cheating with someone else?"

Sociopathic behaviors are so confusing because your expectations about what a romantic relationship is, and how people who are supposed to be in love treat each other, are totally different from those of the sociopath.

You believe that when people are in love, you are good and kind to each other. You treat each other with respect. You support and value each other. You don't lie, and you don't intentionally hurt each other.

Your sociopathic partner, you discover, doesn't share these beliefs. Here's what you need to understand:

1. Sociopaths are fundamentally incapable of love

What is romantic love? You may experience it as a burning desire to be with your beloved, and yes, that's part of it. But scientists have explored this question, and they've identified three components of romantic love.

- The first component is attachment — that's your desire to spend time with your partner.

27

- The second component is sex — which should be self-explanatory.
- The third component is caretaking. If you love some-one, you want to help and protect them. You want them to be happy, healthy and successful. You want what's best for them.

Sociopaths are capable of the first two components — they want to be with you, and they certainly want sex. But they do not do caretaking. Sociopaths cannot be legitimately concerned about someone else's wellbeing. They cannot put someone else's interests before their own. This applies to everyone, including their own children.

The core of sociopathic personality disorders is the inability to love.

2. Sex for a sociopath is only about stimulation

Many people report that sex with the sociopath is the best they've ever had, at least in the beginning of the relationship. If this was your experience, you may have interpreted your earth-shattering sex as an indication of your deep and profound love.

Don't count on it.

Sociopaths are often, although not always, skilled lovers. Here's why:

- All sociopaths, both male and female, have high lev-els of testosterone, which drives them to seek sex.
- All sociopaths crave stimulation, and sex is about the most stimulating of human activities. They start young and engage frequently, so they get a lot of practice.
- Sociopaths have no inhibitions and nothing is off-limits, which can make sex with them very exciting.

For sociopaths, sex has nothing to do with love. They like sex because they want the physical stimulation. They also know that if they can hook someone sexually, it's easier to exploit them.

3. A sociopath's objective is exploitation

You enter a romantic relationship because you want to share love, support and companionship. A sociopath enters a romantic relationship in order to take advantage of you. Right from the very beginning, you are targeted. Here's how this works:

- First, when sociopaths meet you, they figure out if you have something that they want.
- If the answer is yes, they figure out what your vulnerabilities are. They do this by asking deep, probing questions. You feel like they want to know all about you. Actually, they are looking for the deepest place within you to set their hooks.
- Finally, they use your vulnerabilities in order to establish the relationship, and then they convince you to give them what they want.

Remember this: Sociopaths always have an agenda.

4. The sociopath's loving behavior is all an act

In the beginning of an involvement, sociopaths engage in love bombing. They shower you with attention and affection. They tell you how wonderful you are. They want to be with you all the time. While they're still reeling you in, they appear to be kind and considerate.

After some time, you may see flashes of rudeness or anger. The behavior seems out of character, so you assume your partner is simply having a bad day.

Then the sociopath turns on you. You are shocked to find yourself criticized, denigrated and abused. You wonder how the sociopath can suddenly shift from over-the-top affection to complete devaluation.

The truth is that the love and caring you saw in the beginning was a charade designed to hook you. The cruelty and contempt you are seeing now is your partner's true character.

5. Sociopaths only want power and control

Most human beings seek relationships with other people in order to feel connected and attached. We find companionship, support and a sense of community to be intrinsically rewarding.

Sociopaths do not. Sociopaths engage in romantic relationships only to exert power and control over their partners. Sometimes it's a money scam. Sometimes the partners serve as cover for their double lives. Sometimes they initiate romances just for the fun of breaking their partner's hearts.

Sociopaths like being puppeteers. They want to pull the strings and watch other people jump.

This is why the sociopath's behavior in your relationship makes no sense. What the sociopath wants out of the relationship is the total opposite of what you want, and this will never change. That's why, when you realize you're involved with a sociopath, the best solution for you is to get out.

Sociopaths keep changing their demands, keeping you in turmoil

When you're dealing with sociopaths, figuring out what they really want is nearly impossible. Why? Because they keep changing what they want.

When my ex-husband, James Montgomery, moved into my house, I agreed to convert my basement, which I used as a small gym, into an office for him. I put away my gym equipment. I hired builders to install more electric outlets to run his array of computers, televisions and business equipment, which required enclosing the lower part of the walls. Making the improvements, and installing a small bathroom downstairs, cost me $6,000. (He promised to pay me back, but of course he never did.)

When Montgomery first moved into the office, he was delighted.

When we had an argument, he complained about being forced to work out of a dark, dank cellar.

Then, when he was trying to butter me up, he was pleased that "Nuffles" (one of his pet names for me) made such a nice office for him.

Later, as our marriage was falling apart, he again bitterly complained about his deplorable working conditions.

Did Montgomery like the office, or not? I have no idea. The whole issue illustrates how sociopaths will say anything, even directly contradicting themselves, depending on their agenda at the moment.

Moving the goal posts

Many Lovefraud readers have described another, more insidious manifestation of changing sociopathic demands — the phenomenon of continuously "moving the goal posts." Here's how this works:

Sociopaths tell you what they want, which we'll call "A." You give them "A" — except now they want "B." You give them "B," but now they want "C." This can continue for "D," "E" and "F." In fact, it can continue through the entire alphabet, and then through the entire Greek alphabet. Each time, sociopaths insist that this will make them happy.

One target of a sociopath used a different metaphor to describe this behavior — "moving the line in the sand." This person said:

> Moving the line in the sand is a red flag. It serves many purposes. It damages the target. But it also grooms, tests and weakens the target. Plus, the target commits and gets in deeper and deeper to recoup the loss (remember we talked about recouping the loss.) Because it is used to test the target, I think it is an important red flag to look out for.

> The target finds himself/herself tolerating more and more and doing more and more — and the spath does less and less and needs/wants /implicitly demands/expects more and more. Sometimes it's from an overt agreement, sometimes it's from implicit agreements that the line gets moved.

Off balance

What happens to you as they keep changing the rules? You are totally off balance. You can't figure out how to treat them, or how to be around them, because you keep getting mixed signals.

Sociopaths then make matters worse by demeaning you for not doing what they want. You try to explain that you did what they wanted previously, but now they want something different. The sociopaths vociferously deny that they ever told you anything different, and insist that they always wanted what they recently demanded and that you misunderstood them.

Sociopaths are so convincing that you begin to wonder if you did, indeed, misunderstand them, and if you're losing your mind.

Moving the goal posts is a form of gaslighting. It messes with your sense of reality.

Empty inside

Why do sociopaths do this? Why do they keep moving the goal posts?

I think the main reason is that sociopaths are not fully formed human beings — they're empty shells. They have no core personality, no inner fiber, no guiding purpose. Their desires are not based on stable objectives, but passing fancies. They make demands according to whatever they feel like doing in the moment.

Plus they get bored easily. As soon as they tire of one form of entertainment, they want another.

A key question is, do sociopaths do this intentionally? Given that some sociopaths actively try to crush their targets, I certainly think it's possible.

What do you think? Did you experience sociopaths who kept moving the goal posts? If so, were they clueless or doing it in purpose?

10 translations of 'I love you,' when spoken by a sociopath

Most sociopaths are really good at proclaiming their love. They often say the words "I love you" so quickly that it surprises us — how can they already feel that way? We just met!

When we question them, they respond, "You're the one I've been waiting for all my life," or, "I just know that we're perfect for each other," or something equally endearing.

We want to believe them, so we do. They keep pouring it on, until we fall in love with them. The big problem, however, is that our love is real and theirs is fake.

Sociopaths are incapable of love. Even though they sound sincere and convincing, they literally do not have the internal wiring that makes it possible for them to feel authentic love.

So when sociopaths say the words, "I love you," what do they mean? Here are some possibilities:

- I want to have sex with you.
- I want to control you.
- I want to own you.
- I want to sponge off of you.
- I want you to make me look good.
- I want to take advantage of you.
- I want to mess with your mind.
- I want to manipulate you.
- I want to deceive you.
- I want you to serve my needs.

Are the words "I love you," when spoken by a sociopath, a lie? Maybe. Maybe not.

Remember, sociopaths do not experience real love. They do

not know what it is like to truly care about another person's well-being, to give so that another person can flourish. In reality, they have no frame of reference for the word, "love."

Many sociopaths believe that love is sex and sex is love. They like sex. In fact, what sociopaths want in life is power, control and sex.

So if they believe sex and love are synonymous, and say they love you because they want to have sex with you — well, maybe it's the truth.

On the other hand, sociopaths know they are manipulating us. They know we have emotions and they don't, which to them means we have vulnerabilities that they can exploit. Even though they don't feel the words, they have learned that if they say, "I love you," they get what they want.

This is one of the hardest things for the rest of us to come to terms with — that "I love you," when spoken by a sociopath, did not mean what we thought it meant. In fact, the words could have meant nothing at all.

The truth about sex with sociopaths

"Very erotic!" That's how a woman, whom we'll call "Cathy," described the beginning of her relationship with "Matt." "Sex, sex, sex," she said, "and sweet whisperings in my ears."

After a whirlwind romance, they married. Cathy eventually discovered that sex was all Matt really wanted. She found a duffel bag filled with hard-core porn. His sexual demands made her uncomfortable. He cheated. Yet whenever Matt did or said anything hurtful, he soon acted as if nothing had happened.

Matt turned out to be callous, deceitful, manipulative, narcissistic, hostile, irresponsible, reckless and impulsive. In other words, he was a sociopath.

Many people think that sociopaths are all deranged serial killers. In reality, most sociopaths never kill anyone. They are, however, serial exploiters, always on the lookout for someone to use — often for sex.

But you would never know this when you first meet a sociopath. In the beginning, sociopaths seem to be charismatic, charming, exciting — and incredibly sexy.

Rating sex with sociopaths

People who have had sex with individuals that they now believe are sociopaths almost always rave about it. I've spoken to hundreds of people about their experiences. They often tell me that the sex with these individuals was the best they ever had.

For my book, *Red Flags of Love Fraud — 10 signs you're dating a sociopath,* I conducted a survey of more than 1,300 Lovefraud readers. One question was, "If you had sex with the individual, how would you rate it?" Here are the responses:

- Extraordinary — 30%
- Satisfying — 15%
- Dissatisfying — 6%
- At first satisfying, later dissatisfying — 30%
- He/she was satisfied; I was not — 12%
- Abusive — 4%
- Not applicable — 3%

In all, 75% of survey respondents rated the sex as satisfying or more than satisfying, at least in the beginning of the relationship.

Why sociopaths are hot in bed

Sociopaths are hard-wired for sex. They have a lot of energy. They crave excitement and stimulation — it's an integral part of the disorder. Sex, of course, is one of the most stimulating activities a human being can enjoy. Sociopaths want it. They want it early and often. So they start young and engage frequently.

All sociopaths, both male and female, have high levels of testosterone. This hormone drives people to compete for sex partners and then mate with them. In sociopaths, high testosterone means high pursuit.

Besides craving excitement, sociopaths are also born without fear or shame. Consequently, they fail to develop guilt, inhibitions, a conscience or a sense of morality. Social proscriptions against particular acts mean nothing to them. They don't care about the discomfort of their partners either.

So what does all this mean for sociopaths and sex? They have voracious appetites, they indulge often and anything goes.

No feelings of love

You might think that sex with a sociopath sounds exciting. But there are a few more things you should know.

First of all, if you want love along with your sex, you're not going to get it from a sociopath. These people cannot form empathetic connections with other human beings, and therefore are incapable of feeling love. However, they know that if they speak words of love convincingly, they get what they want. So sociopaths

37

often proclaim love quite eloquently — at least until they're bored with you.

Second, if you want to keep the wild sex all for yourself, that's not going to happen either. Most sociopaths cheat. In the Love-fraud survey, 75% of respondents said the sociopaths cheated on them, and 20% said they became infected with a sexually trans-mitted disease.

Finally, sociopaths are not slaves to their testosterone-fueled de-sires. They are quite capable of controlling, even withholding, sex, when it suits their purpose. For these people, sex usually has an agenda. Sometimes it's just the physical release. But often sex is a tool to snare you, so that they can exploit you in some other way.

Sociopaths have incredible sexual magnetism. But if you hook up with them, the excitement will, sooner or later, lead to real problems in your life out of bed.

Sociopathic deception:
A plan or second nature?

Lovefraud received the following important question from a reader:

> When a sociopath targets his victim, does he think and create a plan as to HOW he is going to manipulate his prey to glean what he wants, or is this just second nature to him? How can he spend MONTHS being such a kind, considerate person, going out of his way to do the "little" things that matter in life, before turning into the evil monster?

When you have been deceived and manipulated by a sociopath, the most difficult idea to grasp is how totally different people with this personality disorder are from the rest of us. Their behavior is different from everything we thought we knew about human interaction.

Sociopaths — both male and female — seem to be missing the parts that make the human race human. There is no deep warmth. There is no true caring. There is only fake warmth and fake caring, which disappear immediately once sociopaths decide they have no further use for us.

How do they become like this? According to Dr. Liane Leedom, it's their different motivation.

Power motivation vs. love motivation

Normal people, who do not have a personality disorder, are motivated by both love and power.

We feel emotional love for family, friends, neighbors, and even animals or causes, that are important to us. We care about everything we love, which makes us take action to please, support and protect them.

Normal people also have a healthy power motivation. This is what makes us pursue achievement, leadership and recognition. But our power motivation is kept in check by our love motivation. Therefore, although we strive for accomplishment, we're willing to strive fairly, without injuring other people as we pursue our goals.

In sociopaths, there is no balance between their love motivation and power motivation. The defining characteristic of real love is caring about another person's health and wellbeing, and this is practically nonexistent in sociopaths. Their power motivation, however, is out of control. All they really want is to win, to control and to dominate others.

Born to be manipulative

Sociopathic personality disorders — antisocial, narcissistic and psychopathic — are highly genetic. That means children can be born with a genetic predisposition to the personality disorder. Whether this genetic predisposition "expresses," or becomes active, depends in part on the child's environment, including the parenting he or she receives. When sociopathic parents are part of the child's life, their notoriously bad parenting may encourage their offspring's latent disorder to develop.

When children are born with a genetic predisposition to the personality disorder, what it means in practice is that they have a stronger power motivation than love motivation. From a very early age, these children derive little pleasure from warmth, affection and closeness, and much more enjoyment from getting what they want. Therefore, the children learn, essentially through trial and error, how to behave in order to get what they want. They learn manipulation techniques — and spend their lives perfecting them.

Games sociopaths want to win

To get back to the Lovefraud reader's question, I think sociopaths pursue both avenues of manipulation, depending on the individual and circumstances. Yes, they think and plan about how to get you to deliver what they want. And yes, they've been doing it for so long that much of their behavior is second nature. They are also opportunistic, so when chances to manipulate you pop up, they know exactly how to capitalize on them.

Because their objective is to win, sociopaths view their interactions with you as a game. Some sociopaths have the patience to play the game as long as necessary in order to score that win. Then, when they've achieved their objective, they're finished. The charade is over, and you find, to your horror, that everything the sociopath said and did was designed to deceive you.

How could such
a wonderful young man
turn into an evil sociopath?

Editor's note: Here's a letter Lovefraud received from a reader whom we'll call "Charlotte18." Donna Andersen's response follows the letter.

About a year ago, my husband was arrested for kidnapping a couple of friends of ours. Since then, I have been discovering so many other nefarious things he was doing behind my back, such as stealing money for a living, having relations with other men, committing tax fraud, and the list goes on.

As I look back on our relationship, nearly every one of the items you listed on your checklist rings true for our relationship, but I was very blind to them before his arrest, except for the gaslighting. I called him out on that about three months before his arrest and he responded angrily — that I was crazy and didn't know how good I had it.

So recently, I have been preparing to write an autobiography of my painful experiences, and I've been looking through some of his journaling and writing. (He was a pack rat and kept EVERYTHING. Even writing assignments from grade school, high school and college.) As I've been looking through these, I'm noticing that all of his teachers only had good things to say about him. All of the letters he kept from friends only have praises of his character and amazing friendship. And he always seemed to me to be a wonderful person too, until I looked back at our relationship after his arrest with clearer eyes.

So my question is, can someone be a really good person and healthy psychologically, but then at some point in their adult life become a narcissist or a sociopath? Or is a narcissist always born a narcissist, and he was just able to hide it all through his youth and young adulthood?

We met when he was 19 and married a few years later. He was so very loving and romantic then. Looking back, I can't really pinpoint when things started going downhill, but I'd say it was around 8-10 years into the marriage, so about when he was in his early thirties.

I'm struggling with this, because I know what is truth and I know that our marriage of nearly twenty years was a complete fraud on his part. I found out he was lying to me with absolutely no remorse for the full twenty years about having affairs with other men. But when I look back on his writing and the accolades he received from his teachers and friends, it becomes muddied and confusing.

Donna Andersen responds

Charlotte18,

First of all, I am very sorry for what you are enduring. It is such a shock to find out that everything you believed about your husband, relationship and marriage was a lie.

The subject line of your email asked, "Is he really a narcissist?" Based on what you've described, I think your husband could be diagnosed as having antisocial personality disorder or psychopathy.

All antisocials and psychopaths are also narcissists, but not all narcissists are antisocial or psychopathic. The difference seems to be in the level of malevolence. Narcissists are so focused on their own desires and issues that they don't notice when they hurt other people. Antisocials and psychopaths know they are hurting others, but don't care.

You said that your husband kidnapped people, stole money for a living and committed tax fraud. These are all criminal behaviors — especially kidnapping. Criminal behavior is associated with antisocial personality disorder.

His sexual behavior is also indicative of antisocial personality disorder. Let me be clear — I am not saying that homosexuals are antisocial. I doubt very much that he is homosexual, bisexual or even confused about his sexuality. Sociopaths typically have an extremely strong sex drive. But they also get bored quickly, so many engage in same-sex involvements because they want to manipulate the target, or they simply want to try something new and different.

When you called him out on his gaslighting behavior, he said you were crazy and attacked you. This is a typical disordered response. Nothing is ever their fault. They try to turn the issues around and blame you. When someone blames others for everything that goes wrong, this is a big red flag that you're probably dealing with an antisocial, narcissist or psychopath.

The journals

It's funny that you mention your husband is a pack rat — my ex-husband was also. Not wanting to pry, I never looked through all his file boxes of papers — until I learned that he was cheating on me. When I finally went through his documents, I found evidence of his involvement with 20 to 30 other women — many of whom were asking for their money back.

You found documents from your husband's grade school, high school and college years that were full of praise for him. So I'll summarize your main question as this, "How could a wonderful young man turn into an evil sociopath?"

It is possible that your husband was, indeed, delightful while young. Symptoms of antisocial personality disorder typically appear around puberty. But in some cases, behaviors like lying can be seen in small children, and in other cases the behaviors may not appear until early adulthood. So while most sociopaths exhibit manipulative and exploitative behaviors as teenagers, some do not.

There is also the possibility that your husband was, in fact, disordered at a young age, and had everyone snowed. Last month I posted a link to an article on Quora.com that asked the question: "How do psychopaths behave as children, especially around other children their age?"

Several people who described themselves as psychopaths answered the question. One said, "Behaved very well around my parents and other figures of authority, because behaving well meant that I could get away with more if I were caught." This guy knew exactly what he was doing while young, and maybe your husband did also.

So here's a question for you. Why would your husband even have letters from friends that praise his character and their amazing friendship in the first place? I have several lifelong friends, and although I think they have good opinions of me, none of them has ever written me a letter to express it.

Did your husband ask for these letters? If so, why? Or worse yet, did he write the letters himself?

My psychopathic ex presented me with lots of documentation describing what a successful and heroic man he was. I later found out that it was all forged.

Breaking bad

According to your letter, about eight to 10 years into your marriage, when your husband was in his early 30s, your relationship started going downhill. I'd say that your husband was probably disordered long before then, but he became less worried about keeping his mask in place. Perhaps he felt like he had control over you, so he didn't have to try so hard.

Or, perhaps his bad behavior escalated. Remember, sociopaths get bored. Whatever his misdeeds were when he was young, they were no longer interesting, so to get the same thrill he needed more dangerous behavior. Or, his confidence grew, so he thought he could get away with more.

There is also the possibility that he was always bad, and you simply didn't see it. You were young when you met this man. Perhaps as you matured, you figured out that there was something wrong with his behavior.

What to do today

Everyone who realizes they were involved with a sociopath tries to understand what happened. You try to make sense of the situation, and understanding the disorder is important for that.

But the key now is to realize that there is no treatment and no rehabilitation for personality disorders. Now that your husband is a full-blown sociopath, he will never change. You need to do everything you can to protect yourself and your children.

Dark core of personality: what antisocials, psychopaths, sadists and other miscreants share

Is the disordered person in your life antisocial, narcissistic, borderline, psychopathic — or perhaps even Machiavellian or a sadist?

You may have struggled to figure out which definition applies, perhaps reasoning that a narcissist isn't as bad as a psychopath. In reality, all of these disorders are bad news — people who have them engage in similar destructive behavior.

Now, research from Europe shows that all of these disorders share a common denominator. In a paper called *The Dark Core of Personality*, Ingo Zettler, a psychology professor at the University of Copenhagen, and two German colleagues, define the "D-factor" at the dark core. They write:

> All dark traits can be traced back to the general tendency of placing one's own goals and interests over those of others even to the extent of taking pleasure in hurting others — along with a host of beliefs that serve as justifications and thus prevent feelings of guilt, shame, or the like. The research shows that dark traits in general can be understood as instances of this common core:

- Egoism: an excessive preoccupation with one's own advantage at the expense of others and the community
- Machiavellianism: a manipulative, callous attitude and a belief that the ends justify the means
- Moral disengagement: cognitive processing style that allows behaving unethically without feeling distress
- Narcissism: excessive self-absorption, a sense of su-

periority, and an extreme need for attention from others
- Psychological entitlement: a recurring belief that one is better than others and deserves better treatment
- Psychopathy: lack of empathy and self-control, combined with impulsive behaviour
- Sadism: a desire to inflict mental or physical harm on others for one's own pleasure or to benefit oneself
- Self-interest: a desire to further and highlight one's own social and financial status
- Spitefulness: destructiveness and willingness to cause harm to others, even if one harms oneself in the process

Sociopaths

Lovefraud has long used the term "sociopath" as an umbrella term for people who have any of the various exploitative personality disorders, particularly antisocial, narcissistic and borderline personality disorders, and psychopathy.

Lovefraud periodically catches grief for this. I've been told that I'm using the wrong terminology — sociopath is the old term, and the current term is antisocial personality disorder.

Actually, Lovefraud uses the term "sociopath" as it was originally defined back in 1930.

At that time, a psychologist named George E. Partridge coined the word "sociopathy," and suggested it would be an accurate term for people who are socially maladjusted and motivated towards behavior that adversely affects others. Partridge wrote, "We may use the term 'sociopathy' to mean anything deviated or pathological in social relations."

The American Psychiatric Association created a diagnosis of "sociopathic personality disturbance" in 1952. But in 1968, the diagnosis was replaced with "antisocial personality disorder." Today, the term "sociopath" is no longer an official clinical diagnosis for any psychological disorder.

But this most recent research confirms the validity of identifying a category of people who are exploiters and manipulators.

Yes, they do all engage in similar behavior — but the precise traits and degrees of malevolence vary.

In order to educate the world that people like these exist, a name is needed to describe them. Lovefraud uses "sociopath." It's probably more descriptive than calling them a "D-factor."

Sociopaths, information and power — what you need to know

I clearly remember the words of my sociopathic ex-husband, James Montgomery: "Information is power."

Sociopaths don't really interact with others — they look for ways to exert power and control over the rest of us. Information, Montgomery understood very well, gave him the ability to manipulate, deceive and exploit me and others.

Let's take a close look at how sociopaths acquire and use information at various stages of a romantic relationship.

Advance preparation

If you're looking for romance online, you've probably heard about how to protect yourself when you meet an online date in person. But what's more important is protecting yourself when you create your profile.

When sociopaths are trolling for victims on dating sites, they study online profiles to figure out what you want, and then craft their images to match your wish list. Or, sociopaths present themselves to be just like you, so you feel like you've met your mirror image. What they are doing is using the information that you provide in your dating profile, or on Facebook, Instagram, etc., in order to hook you.

For this reason, limit the amount of information that you reveal in a dating profile or elsewhere online.

When you meet

You may remember that when you first met the sociopath, he or she asked you a lot of questions about yourself, and listened intently to your answers. You probably felt like your new romantic interest was so smitten with you that he or she was hanging on every word.

Actually, the sociopath was probing you to find out if you had anything that he or she wanted. Then, the sociopath listened closely to determine your vulnerabilities, to use them in order to hook you. So once again, the sociopath used information that you provided against you.

During the involvement

The longer you are involved with the sociopath, the more information he or she will amass against you. If you ever let on that you keep a journal, the sociopath will look for it, read it, and perhaps even copy it — yes, I've heard of this happening. The sociopath will go through your computer, phone, drawers, desk, or whatever, looking for information and items that may at some point be useful.

By this time, you may have disclosed many of your deepest fears and secrets to a seemingly sympathetic listener. Once conflict arises, and the sociopath wants to gain the upper hand, you'll find him or her turning your information into ammunition. Anything you've disclosed in confidence will become proof of your inferiority, and therefore justification for the sociopath to attack you.

Break-up

If you're reading Lovefraud, you've begun to figure out what your partner really is, and now you're the one consumed with finding information: Who is this person? What has he or she really been doing all this time? And guess what — for you, information will be hard to come by.

While the sociopath has been drawing information out of you, he or she has been carefully hiding information. Phones and computers are password protected. He or she has been getting the mail first and removing what you aren't supposed to see. Or, perhaps the sociopath even has a post office box that you knew nothing about.

And, when you need information for a divorce or other legal action, it's gone. Mortgage documents, deeds, bank records, your inheritance records — anything you may need as documentation in a court case is missing.

What to do

Here are some tips for protecting your information, which will help you protect your life.

1. If you engage in online dating, do not reveal much information in your profile.
2. When you meet a new dating partner, verify as much information about him or her as you can.
3. In the early stages of a relationship, be cautious about sharing information and be sure that private documents are secure.
4. Once you figure out that you're dealing with a sociopath, keep the information to yourself. Above all, do not confront your partner saying, "I know what you are!"
5. If you are living with the sociopath when you decide to break up, be strategic about your escape, if it's safe to do so. Make copies of all important documents and store them someplace that your soon-to-be-ex doesn't know about.
6. As you prepare to leave, do not let the sociopath know your plans. Keep quiet yourself, and do not reveal your intentions to anyone who the sociopath may pump for information, including your kids.
7. Once the split is underway, be prepared for misinformation. The sociopath will lie to you, and will engage in a smear campaign to convince everyone in your support system that you are mentally unstable and the breakup is entirely your fault. Unfortunately, some people may believe him or her.

The information game

All sociopaths lie, which means they feed you and others false information. They know that if they can convince you to believe their lies, then they have power over you. They may go to elaborate lengths to convince you that their lies are true — creating fraudulent documentation, for example. And of course, when they lie, sociopaths are incredibly convincing.

As my ex-husband said, information is power. Make sure you understand what this means.

11 answers to questions about sociopaths

I heard from a Lovefraud reader who realizes that she's been in a relationship with a sociopath. She's in the phase of trying to wrap her brain around about what these people are, and sent me the following email:

> What happens to these people? These sociopaths? How do they end up in life? Do they just go from victim to victim? Have any of them ever realized the affliction of which they suffer? Do they ever realize they are not capable of love? If they are not capable of love, they will never be happy, right? So...you could present "Red Flags of Love Fraud" to a sociopath and they would not see themselves in it, correct? Do they ever see the error of their ways? There is a rather cryptic site called Narcissism Cured, but that doesn't seem to be possible.
>
> I'm thinking they die alone and unhappy. They don't have the capacity to find true happiness if they don't have the capacity to love. Chemically, what goes on in their brains? Is research being done? Does it run in families?

Many readers, I'm sure, have the same questions, so I'll address them one at a time.

1. What happens to these people? These sociopaths? How do they end up in life?

Many sociopaths eventually crash and burn. But it can take a long time — decades — during which they create havoc for just about everyone in their lives.

There is evidence that sociopaths die younger than people who are not disordered, due to their reckless lifestyle. Even some so-called "successful psychopaths" — those who ply their exploitative trade in the business world — may eventually face a comeuppance. Think Bernie Madoff.

Unfortunately, the sociopath you encountered may never pay directly for what he did to you. You may eventually hear that his life fell apart, that he's burned all his bridges and is in trouble and alone, and you may feel like he got what he deserved.

But don't wait for it. You need to find your own way of getting past what happened, so that you can move on.

2. Do they just go from victim to victim?

Yes. Sociopaths live their lives by exploiting people. They view every social interaction as a feeding opportunity.

3. Have any of them ever realized the affliction of which they suffer?

Yes, some of them realize that they are sociopaths. I have heard from people who tell me they've been diagnosed with the disorder. Some of them seem to be perturbed — they're probably the ones who are fairly low on the sociopathic scale.

Others view themselves as superior beings. They don't view sociopathy as an affliction. Rather, they see it as a competitive advantage.

4. Do they ever realize they are not capable of love?

Some of them know they are missing something. But having never experienced love, they don't quite know what it is. It's like asking someone who is colorblind to describe red or green. They have no frame of reference.

5. If they are not capable of love, they will never be happy, right?

Sociopaths are motivated by three things: power, control and sex. So when they feel like they have power and control, or when they successfully pursue sex, they would probably describe themselves as happy.

6. So...you could present "Red Flags of Love Fraud" to a sociopath and they would not see themselves in it, correct?

They may very well recognize their behavior. But they probably won't see anything wrong with it.

7. Do they ever see the error of their ways?

Sociopaths feel totally entitled to do whatever they want to get whatever they want. So if you hear words like, "I'm sorry," "I know I've treated you badly," or "It's all my fault," well, they are not expressing genuine remorse. They're worming their way back into your life so they can exploit you again.

8. There is a rather cryptic site called Narcissism Cured, but that doesn't seem to be possible.

All antisocials are narcissists, although not all narcissists are antisocials. The difference appears to be in the degree of malevolence. Narcissists are so focused on themselves that they don't notice when they hurt people. Antisocials often hurt people intentionally.

Once an antisocial is an adult, there is no proven cure. I think the same thing applies to narcissists.

It may be possible for someone with a personality disorder to learn to control the expression of his or her disorder. But keeping a lid on bad behavior doesn't mean the disorder is cured.

9. I'm thinking they die alone and unhappy. They don't have the capacity to find true happiness if they don't have the capacity to love.

Perhaps. They may also live by the motto, "He who dies with the most toys wins."

10. Chemically, what goes on in their brains? Is research being done?

There are chemical and structural differences in the brains of psychopaths (the term used by most academic researchers). There are also differences in the ways that parts of psychopaths' brains communicate with each other.

Research is ongoing. Maybe the scientists will eventually find a way to change the brain to correct the disorder. But will a psychopath submit to treatment? If they don't believe there is anything wrong with them, why should they?

11. Does it run in families?

Psychopathy is highly genetic. This means children may be born with a predisposition for the disorder. Whether the disorder actually develops has much to do with environmental factors, especially the parenting that the individual receives.

If a person is born with the genes for psychopathy, if often means that one of the parents is disordered. Unfortunately, psychopaths make terrible parents, so conditions are usually ripe for their children to also become disordered. In fact, some psychopaths intentionally try to turn their children into little Mini-Me's.

That's why it's so important to understand the Red Flags of Love Fraud. Becoming romantically involved with these individuals always has the potential of leading to children — children who may also become disordered.

5 reasons why antisocials are great actors

Lovefraud published an article by Eleanor Cowan entitled, *When sociopaths use righteous indignation to exert control*. In it, Eleanor relates how her fiancé twisted her comment about a pedophile priest into an opportunity to establish his moral superiority over her. The fiancé, of course, was disordered and a pedophile himself, but Eleanor didn't know it at the time. He convinced her that he was a righteous, religious man.

A Lovefraud reader commented on the post:

> This article really is a perfect example of how they manipulate you – what I want to know is HOW is it they are so believable? How come they are such good actors?? I would think the average non-sociopathic person would be unable to lie as convincingly as an actual sociopath because a sociopath has no conscience, but what I want to understand is how come they are SUCH great actors?

In answer to our reader's questions, keep in mind what acting is. It is lying. Actors try to convince us that they are the people they portray, and that they really mean all the things they say in their lines. This is exactly what sociopaths do. The difference is in the intent. With actors, everyone knows that they are just telling a story for our entertainment. With sociopaths, we, the targets, are being duped.

Here are five reasons why people with antisocial personality disorder or psychopathy are such believable actors. Four of them are about the disordered individuals, and one is about us, the targets.

1. Lying without anxiety

All antisocials lie. This is a cardinal trait of the disorder. They tell big lies, little lies, outrageous lies, stupid lies. Of course, we all lie from time to time, perhaps to spare someone's feelings or get out of trouble. But most normal people do not lie with anywhere near the fluency of an antisocial or psychopath.

The key to antisocial success in deception is that they do not feel anxiety when they lie. How can they do this? It's rooted in their sense of entitlement. These people feel entitled to get what they want, when they want it and how they want it. If lying is required to meet their objectives, that's just fine with them.

Therefore, antisocials and psychopaths do not show any of the physical symptoms of lying. Their heart rate and blood pressure do not increase; their breathing does not change; they do not sweat. These are the physical changes measured by polygraph machines — which antisocials and psychopaths routinely beat.

All those "tells" that people are lying — like looking away or failing to make eye contact — do not work with antisocials and psychopaths.

2. Glibness and superficial charm

Most antisocials and psychopaths are born with silver tongues. They always have an answer, never miss a beat. The ability to talk smoothly is simply a trait of the disorder. In fact, the first item in Dr. Robert Hare's Psychopathy Checklist Revised, the prime tool for diagnosing psychopaths, is "glibness and superficial charm."

Those of us with normal verbal skills may hesitate or reach for words when trying to express ourselves. Antisocials and psychopaths speak without hesitation, whether they're love bombing us or coming up with an excuse. Because their words come so smoothly, we interpret their statements to be true.

3. Changing like chameleons

Antisocials and psychopaths have no internal core. They have no real values, no ideals beyond going after whatever they want in the moment. This is what enables them to be chameleons. They can change their colors, totally reinventing themselves, depending on whom they are interacting with.

Again, this makes them great actors. What do actors do? They take on a role, and try to get us to believe their portrayal.

Disordered individuals who are pursuing romantic partners typically figure out what the target is looking for, make themselves into that person, and then proclaim that they are soul mates. The targets believe they've met the partners they've been waiting for all their lives, when actually the antisocials and psychopaths are just mirroring their own traits.

4. Practice makes perfect

Exploitative personality disorders typically emerge during the teenage years, although sometimes traits — like lying — can be seen in young at-risk children. Therefore, most antisocials and psychopaths have been manipulating others — by lying and acting — all their lives. The more they do it, the better they get at it.

As they get older, antisocials may realize that they aren't like other people. But they also know that in order pursue their agenda, whatever it is, they need to fit in. Sometimes they actually study how people react in situations requiring empathy so they can learn what to do.

By the time you meet adult antisocials and psychopaths, they've perfected their craft.

5. Humans are lousy lie detectors

According to a meta-analysis of 253 research studies, human beings can identify a lie only about 53% of the time — not much better than flipping a coin.

I imagine that those 253 research studies involved mostly controlled environments with college students lying to each other. What happens when skilled antisocials and psychopaths are lying to their romantic partners?

We are biologically programmed to trust people. Whenever we share intimacy with someone — and a hug or conversation qualifies as intimacy — our bodies release a shot of oxytocin. This neurotransmitter facilitates trust. It makes us feel calm, trusting and content, and it alleviates fear and anxiety.

So if your disordered partner is putting on an act, he or she is naturally talented and has years of practice. You, being a normal, trusting human, are primed to believe it. That's why it all seems so real.

Think of sociopaths as aliens — it may help you understand them

Perhaps the hardest thing to comprehend, and accept, about sociopaths is just how different they are from the rest of us.

I've spoken to hundreds of people who have tangled with sociopaths. Even when the mask has not only slipped, but shattered, even when they know the truth about what the sociopath has been doing all along, they still ask,

- "But how could he do it?"
- "He kept telling me how much he loved me; how could he cheat like that?"
- "He said we were soul mates; how can he just up and leave?"
- "How can he be so cold and calculating?"
- "How can he look me right in the eye and lie?"

(Substitute "she" for "he" as necessary.)

Then, the people I talk to start making statements like the following:

- "I would never think of taking someone's money."
- "I would never intentionally hurt someone."
- "If I said something like that, I couldn't sleep at night."
- "I would never tell someone that I loved them if I didn't mean it."

So here is the most important lesson to learn about sociopaths: You cannot interpret their behavior in the same way you interpret your own behavior.

Understanding the Sociopath

Sociopaths are fundamentally different from the rest of us. They have a personality disorder, and this disorder reaches to the core of their beings. Here's what this means:

- Sociopaths cannot feel empathetic connections with other people.
- Sociopaths do not have the ability to love.
- Sociopaths are interested only in power, control and sex.
- Sociopaths' main motivation is to win.
- Anything that comes out of a sociopath's mouth could be a lie.
- Sociopaths have no conscience.

You could think of them as aliens. I'm not saying that they literally are aliens (although there are people who believe that). But sociopaths are missing the characteristics, traits and abilities that make us truly human.

For most of us, this realization is a shock to the system. They look just like the rest of us. They appear to be so normal, talented, fun and exciting. They keep proclaiming their love. It's so hard to believe that they are simply acting. It's all a charade, a mirage.

What do you do with this information? You accept it. Sociopaths are what they are, and once they are adults, there is nothing you or anyone else can do about it. So far, there is no therapy, no magic pill, which will give them the ability to feel care and concern for others, or internalize a sense of right and wrong.

All we can do is know that they exist, learn the warning signs, and when we see them, run as fast as we can.

One trait or behavior does not make a sociopath – look for a pattern of traits and behaviors

I once heard from a man, whom we'll call "Jeff," who wanted to know if the woman he was involved with, "Amanda," was a sociopath.

It started as a friendly involvement, with Jeff trying to help Amanda out. Amanda, who was from a foreign country, called Jeff her "best friend." Jeff eventually started to have feelings for her. But then came a series of unsettling experiences:

Amanda made pornographic videos, which were posted on the Internet.

Amanda worked as an escort. Jeff offered to pay her rent, so she wouldn't have to be an escort, and Amanda agreed — and continued being an escort anyway.

Then Jeff asked Amanda to sign a contract promising that she wouldn't be an escort. She signed it — and broke the deal again, with absolutely no guilt.

Amanda claimed to be struggling financially. Although Jeff wasn't well off, he gave her money — and then discovered that Amanda sent a large sum of money back to her home country.

Jeff discovered Amanda was having multiple liaisons, often on the same day. One guy was married, one was a "sugar daddy," and several were her "best friend."

Other men were also paying her phone bill and rent.

Jeff stopped taking her calls, but did communicate via email. They agreed to get together to "talk things over." Amanda cancelled.

When they did finally have a conversation, Jeff thought Amanda's words sounded hollow. He also realized her words were used for manipulation, not for communicating the truth.

Jeff stopped talking to Amanda. But he knew that if he contacted her again, she would be nice and friendly, as if nothing ever happened.

So is Amanda a sociopath? I think so, and that's what I told Jeff.

His next question was, "What are the most glaring indications that she is a sociopath?"

And that brings us to the point of this article: The most glaring indication of sociopathy is not any particular trait or behavior, but the overall pattern of traits and behaviors.

Sociopathy is a syndrome. What exactly does that mean? Here's the Dictionary.com definition:

> Pathology, Psychiatry — a group of symptoms that together are characteristic of a specific disorder, disease, or the like.

So, although Amanda is an escort, it doesn't necessarily make her a sociopath. She took advantage of Jeff, but that doesn't make her a sociopath. She had multiple sexual relationships, but that doesn't make her a sociopath. Her words sounded hollow, but that doesn't make her a sociopath. And, if Jeff and Amanda ever talked again, she would act as if nothing happened, but that doesn't make her a sociopath.

Amanda is a sociopath because of her overall traits and pattern of behavior, including promiscuity, entitlement, manipulation, exploitation, breaking agreements, lying, shallow emotions and lack of remorse. All of these characteristics, taken together, add up to character disorder.

Will the sociopath treat the next wife better?

Lovefraud received the following email from a divorced reader:

I always knew there was something wrong with my ex-husband, and friends and family did as well. There were lies, gambling, cheating, drug use, rehab 3 times, head games. He would drive erratically with our son and I in the car (even when our son was very little). He would speed up if there were a cat or other animal in the road. I would always completely freak out so he never ran one over when I was in the car, but I wouldn't be surprised if he did when I wasn't. (I could tell his counselor in rehab #3 knew there was more to his problems than just drug addiction.) He was clean for a long time and that's when I realized it wasn't the drugs. He has always been able to get his way and talk people into things. I always made excuses and actually made myself believe he would grow out of it as he got older. But I did not pinpoint what "it" was until discovering Lovefraud.

I've been divorced for over 2 years now and my ex-husband is remarried to someone with 2 young teenage children. I sometimes get obsessed thinking about whether or not they are happy. I often wonder if he's better to her than he was to me. I know our 22-year-old son feels somewhat replaced and like his father just moved right on with no problem (which I know is typical of a sociopath). I guess I need some reassurance about sociopaths in second marriages from experts to put my mind at rest. My ex has a history of lying, cheating, drug use (actually got more sociopathic after he got clean and sober for over 8 years). About 6 months before I filed for divorce, he told me he gets a rush out of getting away with things and it's gone on since he was a kid and he doesn't know why. I just want to know that his new marriage is not all candy and roses. Can you address sociopaths in new marriages on your site? While I know I sound a little pathetic, I think it may help many.

Put your mind at ease: Your ex-husband does not love his new wife. He will never love his new wife. The reason is quite simple: Sociopaths are incapable of love.

Acting the part

Now, they are quite capable of acting like they are in love. They can give a command performance of heartfelt sentiments and promises of endless fidelity. But it is an act, and when the partner no longer serves a purpose for the sociopath, the act will end.

The new wife, of course, does not know this. So while your ex-husband is acting like he is in love, the new wife may legitimately be in love. She may be happy. She may be thrilled. She may believe that she's found the person she's been waiting for all her life, and all her dreams have come true.

Your ex-husband will nurture her dreams, at least while she still has something that he wants, which could be money, a place to live, or a facade of normalcy should he start using drugs again. After all, he gets a rush out of getting away with things — like deceiving the new wife.

Truth revealed

Eventually he will revert to his true, miserable self. But even as the wife starts to see the same lies, gambling, cheating and drug use that you saw, for a time she will overlook the behavior, or support her man as he goes for a fourth round of rehab. For a time she will continue to believe the act.

Sooner or later, however, your ex-husband's mask will slip again, or he will completely remove it. When she sees the truth, she will experience the same pain, devastation and betrayal that you experienced.

He is what he is.

You need to get to the point where you thoroughly understand that he is what he is, and he will always be what he is. A snake is always a snake. He will not be a snake with you and a teddy bear with her.

Your ex-husband is a sociopath. Sociopaths are fundamentally different from the loving and empathetic people who make up the rest of the human race, and there is nothing you or anyone else can do about it. If you think of them as aliens, you aren't far off.

Once you viscerally understand this, your obsession should come to an end.

Naming the social predators
among us

How do you avoid a social predator? First, you have to know that they exist.

I didn't know they existed. So when a charming, charismatic and supremely confident man swept into my life, I didn't know that charm, charisma and overconfidence were red flags that he might be a predator. And he was. This man took a quarter-million dollars from me, cheated with at least six women during our 2.5-year marriage, had a child with one of the women, and then, 10 days after I left him, married the mother of the child. It was the second time he committed bigamy.

"He might be a sociopath," my therapist commented, as I described his mind-boggling betrayal and duplicity.

Sociopath? I thought a sociopath was a serial killer.

Well, not necessarily. Sociopaths are people who routinely exploit and manipulate others. But you'd never know it to meet them. Sociopaths are not delusional, and they do not necessarily look like thugs. In fact, they blend easily into society and often have good social skills. Like the man I married, they are frequently charming, charismatic and confident.

And they are a huge problem. Experts estimate that 1% to 4% of the population are antisocial or psychopathic — two varieties of sociopaths. That means there are 3 million to 12 million of them in the United States. Plus, additional millions have sociopathic traits but not the full disorder.

Back in 2005, I launched Lovefraud.com to educate the public about these disordered individuals. My first problem was deciding how to refer to them.

Multiple diagnoses

In the mental health field, social predators may be called sociopaths, psychopaths, narcissists or antisocials, depending upon whom you ask. Borderlines and histrionics engage in similar behavior.

Research psychologists tend to use the term "psychopath," whereas clinicians and counselors use the diagnoses in the American Psychiatric Association *Diagnostic and Statistical Manual (DSM)* — the bible of mental health conditions and illnesses. These diagnoses are antisocial, narcissistic, borderline and histrionic personality disorders.

The DSM once referred to "sociopathic personality disturbance," but that was changed to "antisocial personality disorder." Psychiatrists and clinicians tend to use "sociopath" as a shorthand way of referring to a person with the condition. At least, that's the current usage. The psychiatrists have updated their manual and have suggested yet another name for this disorder: "antisocial/psychopathic type." (Try using that in a sentence.)

In addition to disagreeing about the name, experts also argue about what the names mean.

- Some consider a "psychopath" to be an extreme form of "sociopath."
- Some say "psychopath" describes personality traits and "sociopath" describes behavior.
- Some see this as a nature vs. nurture issue—"psychopaths" are born, "sociopaths" are the result of bad parenting and deprivation.
- Some people use the terms depending on how a person is diagnosed. If psychiatric standards are used, the person is a "sociopath." If the Psychopathy Checklist Revised (PCL-R), a standardized evaluation, is used, the person is a "psychopath."
- Some think of a sociopath as someone who is socialized into an antisocial subculture, such as a gang.

In short, naming this disorder is a mess. And as the experts argue, the public is in the dark.

Confusion in the general public

Lovefraud.com gets 100,000 visitors a month, and I've collected more than 10,000 cases of people involved with sociopaths. We once surveyed our readers and asked a few questions about the name of the disorder. More than 1,200 people responded. Here are the questions and the results:

"Before your involvement with this disordered individual, what did you understand the term 'sociopath' to mean?"

- Criminal — 19%
- Serial killer — 19%
- Someone who was delusional — 6%
- Person without empathy or a conscience — 20%
- I didn't know what it meant — 35%

"Before your involvement with this disordered individual, what did you understand the term 'psychopath' to mean?"

- Criminal — 15%
- Serial killer — 51%
- Someone who was delusional —13%
- Person without empathy or a conscience — 9%
- I didn't know what it meant — 12%

So, half of the readers thought "psychopath" meant serial killer, and the largest number of responses for "sociopath" was "I didn't know what it meant."

No support in the aftermath

Why is this discussion important? Why should anyone care about what to call people who lie, cheat, steal and abuse?

Two reasons: First of all, these social predators are probably responsible for most of the manmade misery in the world, ranging from the fraud perpetrated by Ponzi schemers, to the abusers who force their partners into domestic violence shelters, to the bullies causing turmoil in the workplace.

Secondly, once you become entangled with a sociopath, there is usually no support from legal, financial or other institutions. Why? Because most sociopaths use social interactions to find and exploit their targets. This means there is some kind of relationship between the predator and the victim, which muddies the water when the victim seeks redress.

The only effective way to deal with the trauma caused by social predators is prevention. Prevention requires education. And for education to work, we need agreement on what to call these people.

This is a medical disorder

It is not sufficient to say that these predatory individuals are "abusers" or "toxic." We are talking about a medical disorder, a mental condition, not merely a lifestyle choice. Of all the personality disorders, only these are defined by the affected individual's victimization of others. The perpetrators themselves rarely experience distress because of their actions. It is the people around them who experience distress.

Mental health professionals, searching for possible causes and treatment, engage in nuanced debates with each other about definitions and diagnostic criteria. For example, are antisocial personality, narcissism and psychopathy distinct disorders, or are they different points on the same continuum of abusive behavior? In practice, the behaviors and traits exhibited by individuals diagnosed with psychopathy, sociopathy, narcissism and even borderline personality disorders overlap, so it's hard to tell where one ends and another begins.

From the perspective of those of us who have tangled with one of these individuals, however, the clinical diagnosis doesn't matter. Our lives were turned upside down, we lost money, our homes, our children. We suffered PTSD or other maladies. The point is that we were involved with a disordered person, and we were damaged.

Proposal for a name

When it comes to helping people avoid exploitative personalities, it's not a diagnostic issue, but an education and communications issue.

I propose a solution for the name problem. I propose that "sociopathy" be used as a generic, layman's term, similar to "heart disease." It would not be a clinical diagnosis. It would be a general description of a personality disorder in which the people who have the disorder purposely exploit others.

Let's compare it to "heart disease." There are various types of heart disease, like a heart attack, or, clinically speaking, a myocardial infarction. There's also cardiovascular disease, coronary artery disease, and so on. The American Heart Association tells us to keep our heart healthy by not smoking, avoiding fatty foods, and getting regular exercise. They don't tell us to avoid heart attacks by doing this, or avoid strokes by doing that. They provide information to protect the whole system.

With my suggestion, under the umbrella of "sociopathy," the professionals could determine actual clinical diagnoses. They may decide that a "psychopath" should be defined as someone who scores 30 or more on the PCL-R. A "narcissist" should be someone with an overactive sense of entitlement. "Antisocial personality disorder" should describe the people who routinely violate the rights of others. Other subcategories could be defined as the experts see fit.

The idea here is coming up with a general term that describes social predators so that people can be educated. It doesn't matter if someone is diagnosed to be a narcissist, sociopath or psychopath. The idea is to avoid all of them.

Understanding the red flags

I've talked to and corresponded with hundreds of people who have tangled with these exploiters. Time after time I've heard, "I never knew that people like this existed." This is the problem that needs to be solved—alerting the public that social predators exist. To do this effectively, one agreed-upon term is necessary.

"Sociopath" has the advantage of already being in the lexicon, without the cultural baggage of "psychopath." People are generally aware that the word has something to do with bad behavior towards others. But, as our survey pointed out, most people don't really know what "sociopath" means, so they can be educated.

In another Lovefraud survey about romantic relationships involving sociopaths, 71% of people said that they had a gut feeling or intuition early in the relationship that the individual was bad news. Most people said they ignored their internal warnings and continued the relationship. Why? I think a big reason is because they did not have the empirical knowledge that sociopaths existed. They saw the red flags and did not know what they meant, so they dismissed them.

In my view, settling on a clear name for this disorder, or range of disorders, is a public health issue. People have learned how to protect themselves from heart disease. Sociopaths cause physical, emotional and psychological injury, illness and trauma. We need to learn how to protect ourselves from them.

Can the ill effects from tangling with these predators be totally avoided? Probably not. But if we know that sociopaths exist, and know the warning signs of exploitative behavior, we may be able to escape before too much damage is done.

10 reasons why sociopaths' lies seem so believable

When we finally figure out that just about everything a sociopath told us is a lie, we are shocked. How can anyone lie so fluently? And why did we fall for it?

Here are 10 reasons why the lies sociopaths tell seem so believable:

1. Sociopaths tell you how honest they are

Early on, sociopaths may tell you how much they value honesty, that truthfulness is the foundation of all relationships. Their objective is to convince you of their trustworthiness, so that when you encounter their lies, you don't see them.

2. Sociopaths lie while they look directly into your eyes

Some experts say that if people look up and to their right while speaking, it's a sign that they are lying. Other experts dispute this. Regardless, we all tend to believe that if someone can look us in the eye while talking, then they are telling the truth. Sociopaths know this, so they look us in the eye as they lie.

3. Sociopaths mix truth with lies

This is a key sociopathic strategy — mixing truth with lies. You know for a fact that some of what the sociopath says is true (and the sociopath knows that you know), so you infer that the rest is true. Unfortunately, you're wrong.

4. Everything is a lie

One way that we spot lies is by noticing change. At first, the story was this, now it's that. With a sociopath, however, there is no change to notice, because the lying starts from the very beginning and just keeps going.

5. Sociopaths lie with no physical reaction

Lying makes most of us feel anxious, which causes physical symptoms. These symptoms are what polygraph machines measure — changes in heart rates/blood pressure, respiration and skin conductivity. Because sociopaths are comfortable lying, they feel no anxiety, so there are no physical changes to observe.

6. Sociopaths cover their lies with more lies

When we confront sociopaths about their lies, they tell more lies to cover up the original lies. Most of us would never be able to keep all the lies straight, but sociopaths are frequently gifted in this — they can remember exactly what they told to whom, and they keep the story going.

7. "I would never lie!"

When questioned about something they said, sociopaths often proclaim, with righteous indignation, that they would never lie. They are so emphatic about this, and so obviously crestfallen that you could possibly think that they lied, that you end up apologizing — even though they are, in fact, lying.

8. Sociopaths lie with complete confidence

It's hard to imagine that someone who is so charismatic, charming and confident is also a complete liar. They exhibit no doubt whatsoever. They seem to command you to believe them — so you do.

9. The claims are so outrageous that they must be true

Sociopaths claim to be Special Forces soldiers, foreign royalty, Ph.D. scientists, born-again Christians, spiritual leaders and more. They may forge or buy certificates, medals and other documentation to prove their stories. You can't imagine anyone would have the nerve to make such claims without them being true — so you believe them.

10. Practice makes perfect, and sociopaths practice a lot

The more sociopaths lie, the better they get at it — and typically, sociopaths have been lying all their lives. So they are very, very good liars. Unfortunately, most humans are lousy lie detectors, so the rest of us simply haven't got a chance. Sociopaths lie, and we don't spot the lies — until it's too late.

Explaining evil —
the psychopathic agenda

Evil does, in fact, exist. That was the revelation posted by Richard Cohen, a columnist with the Washington Post.

The impetus for his column was the atrocities committed by the Islamic State — the jihadists who overran Iraq, murdered anyone they didn't like, and beheaded American photojournalist James Foley.

"I used to not believe in evil," Cohen wrote in his article, *The Islamic State is evil returned*. Now he does.

Cohen compares the acts committed by the Islamic State to those of other purveyors of brutal atrocities — Adolph Hitler and the Nazis. In the generations since World War II, Cohen notes, philosophers and editorial writers have obsessed over the question: "Why?" Why did the Nazis inflict such horrors on other people?

Cohen quotes the conclusion of another writer, Martin Amis: There is no why.

The why: Psychopaths

On the contrary, I believe there is an explanation for evil actions, like those committed by the Nazis and Islamic State jihadists.

The people who come up with diabolical plans for mass murder and other atrocities are psychopaths.

Here's the key point to understand about psychopaths: They are fundamentally different from the rest of us. They are literally missing the trait that makes the rest of us human.

Psychopaths have no ability to love.

This is the point so many people asking "why?" fail to get. They are trying to interpret evil behavior through a normal lens. They ask how any normal person can do what these tyrants and murderers do.

The answer is that psychopaths are not normal.

Human motivation

Human beings experience four social motivations:

- Attachment — the desire to be with people, especially a significant other
- Sex
- Caretaking — a desire to look out for and take care of other people. This is the essence of real love for another person.
- Power — the desire for a superior social position.

The first three motivations — attachment, sex and caretaking — are the three components of romantic love.

The fourth motivation —power — isn't necessarily bad in measured doses. After all, it's our power motivation that makes us want to be achievers and leaders.

According to Dr. Liane Leedom, in normal people, the power motivation is held in check by our love motivation. We want to secure power and social position for ourselves, but not at the expense of severely hurting someone else.

Psychopaths, however, are totally different.

Psychopaths, Dr. Leedom explains, have no love motivation to put the brakes on their power motivation. They experience power and control as totally exhilarating, and don't experience love and the desire to care for others at all.

So psychopaths have an out-of-control desire for power, with no concern about what happens to others. That means a psychopath can do whatever he or she wants to pursue domination, and experiences no guilt or remorse about steamrolling anyone who is in the way.

Gathering followers

Widespread atrocities, such as those committed by the Nazis

and Islamic State, require the involvement of many people. How do all these people get involved?

First of all, the leaders of evil movements are likely to be psychopaths. Saddam Hussein was a psychopath, according to his personal physician. Most people consider Adolph Hitler to be a psychopath, although he may have had other mental issues as well. Cult leaders are probably all psychopaths.

We know first hand how convincing and manipulative psychopaths are. They convince other people to go along with their plans. In the beginning they are magnetic and charming, but later, as their power increases, psychopaths may increasingly use tactics of fear and brutality.

So what happens to the followers?

Many of the followers may have psychopathic traits themselves. The more disordered they are, the more they are willing to do the leader's dirty work.

Psychopathy is also, in a way, contagious.

High levels of aggressive and brutal behavior reinforce an individual's power motivation, and weaken the caretaking motivation. So people who already had psychopathic traits become worse. And those who perhaps did not have psychopathic traits, but cooperated with the evil movement in order to survive, lose their humanity and become more callous.

Finally, some people in the movements are brainwashed — especially those who started becoming indoctrinated while young, like the Hitler youth and many boys educated in jihadist madrassas.

Dealing with evil

Here's another article about conditions on the ground in Iraq: *'They're so evil': Pastor serving in Iraq says Islamic State's murderous rampage like nothing 'seen since the days of the Holocaust,'* posted on TheBlaze.com.

So what does this all mean for the international community?

Leaders whose job it is to make national and international policy need to know what we know about dealing with psychopaths:

- They lie.
- They cannot be trusted.
- They will promise anything, then do what they want.
- Their sole objective is winning.
- If you give them one inch they will take 10 miles.
- You cannot appeal to their humanity, because they have none.
- They do not care who gets hurt, or killed, including their own.

All of us at Lovefraud know what's like to have a psychopath wreak havoc in our lives. Unfortunately, psychopaths are also capable of wreaking havoc on a grand scale.

The world is dealing with evil. I hope our leaders who are deciding how to respond recognize that.

If a sociopath cries at movies, does it mean he has feelings?

*L*ovefraud received the following email from a reader whom we'll call "Alana."

Thank you for this wonderful site. Unless you have been through it, no one can understand the insanity of a Narcissist/psychopath.

There are three things that I have noticed about my Narcissist.

1. He can cry at movies, at cute you tube videos about kittens, but if I am upset, he stares at me blankly. I understand that he does not have any empathy toward me, but what is the deal with the crying at movies, etc? You know, for a long time I thought that was a sign that he really did have feelings that would eventually show themselves. That he had the capacity for empathy. But I was so wrong. How is this possible?

2. I read somewhere that Covert Narcissists are "empty" people. I had to sit down when I read that. They don't really have any passions in life. They live in a space of "ho hum." No real goals, never really finish anything they start, like to hoard because one day they are going to get to that. This describes my current ex and my mother. Empty. Languid. Sorta sad. Lost. What are your thoughts on this?

3. Very concrete. In the movie, *This is where I leave you,* (which offers great portrayals of Narcissism), Justin Bateman says to Dax Sheppard's character, "You know, until I met you, I thought I was the biggest loser." Now this is not a compliment. But Dax Sheppard's character says, "Thank you." I have seen this in my own life. It is like they are not paying attention to what is being said, or they don't get the nuance that this is not a compliment. What is going on here?

Donna Andersen responds

Before I address Alana's questions, I want to lay some groundwork.

We all know that there is an infinite variety of people in the world. People all have different traits, behaviors, virtues, faults, habits, strengths, weaknesses, passions and fears.

This applies to disordered people as well. Even when psychopaths, antisocials, narcissists and borderlines are all diagnosed as disordered, they can still exhibit an extremely wide range of traits and behaviors.

More formally, psychopathy is considered to be a "syndrome" and a "continuum."

A "syndrome" is a collection of traits, characteristics or symptoms that tend to cluster together. The key symptoms of a psychopath, for example, include glib and superficial, egocentric and grandiose, lack of remorse or guilt, lack of empathy, deceitful and manipulative, and shallow emotions, plus indications of an antisocial lifestyle.

Many psychopaths are glib, meaning they have really good social skills. They always seem to know what to say and have an answer for everything. My ex-husband was charismatic and charming. But plenty of readers have told me that the disordered individuals they were involved with had no social skills at all.

That's where the "continuum" idea comes it. Any particular psychopath or narcissist can have any of the traits to a greater or lesser degree. In fact, just about all of these traits, in smaller doses, may be considered to be normal.

For example, most of us lie from time to time. We usually have a reason, such as getting out of trouble or sparing somebody's feelings. Psychopaths, however, lie all the time, and often just for the fun of it. So lying once in awhile is normal, but constant lying is pathological. It's a matter of degree.

So let's take a look at Alana's questions.

Crying

Many psychopaths and other disordered individuals are great actors and can turn on the tears at will. However, they many not always know when it is appropriate to start crying.

The man Alana is describing may have learned, through observation, that crying at certain movies and videos is appropriate. But if he is disordered and lacks empathy, he may be unable to register Alana's distress, or can't be bothered with responding.

If this is the case, crying at a sad movie is an act, and failing to respond appropriately when Alana is crying is the truth of his personality.

Empty people

Psychopaths, sociopaths and narcissists are usually empty when it comes to emotions. Typically the range of emotions they experience is very narrow — limited to negative emotions such as anger, rage and jealousy.

Psychopaths and narcissists do not experience love. That is the core of the disorder.

But plenty of psychopaths and narcissists have passions — just not the same passions as the rest of us. They have a passion for power and control. They may pursue money, sex or notoriety.

Yes, many psychopaths do not finish what they start — but some of them do. And yes, I've heard of other psychopaths who are hoarders — but certainly not all of them have this trait.

So I'd say that disordered people are empty, but this doesn't always manifest in the same way.

Nuance

About Alana's observation about a person who doesn't get the nuance of a statement — as an isolated behavior, this may or may not be related to a personality disorder. But if Alana is seeing other traits and behaviors linked to psychopathy or narcissism in the individual, it could just be an example of the general disconnect between disordered individuals and the rest of us.

So here's the take-home message: Disordered individuals are not all the same. They may have the various traits linked to personality disorders to greater or lesser degrees. What's important is to look at the overall picture. If you see most of the behavior patterns that we talk about here on Lovefraud, get the person out of your life.

9 reasons why sociopaths blow your mind

When you finally figure out that you're dealing with sociopaths, your state of mind is complete and utter shock. On the one hand, you are relieved to know that it's not you; something is definitely wrong with them. On the other hand, you still can't wrap your brain around their behavior.

It's mind-boggling, and here's why:

1. Everything you believed was a lie

You probably caught some of the lies as you went along, but the sociopaths explained them away. Then you learned that the entire nature of your involvement, the entire reason they are in your life, is complete fabrication. It was never about romance, or shared goals, or family. It was about exploitation.

2. The unbelievable sense of entitlement

Not only do the sociopaths exploit you and everyone else, they feel totally entitled to do it. They want what they want, when they want it and how they want it. Other people are simply tools to get them what they want. Why? Because in the mind of the sociopaths, that's what they deserve.

3. The mask comes off, and you don't know who is behind it

They were so charming, so helpful, so caring — and they're gone. Now the sociopaths treat you with disdain — criticizing, belittling, ignoring and abusing you. You wonder what happened to the sweetness and chivalry — and realize it was all a charade, an act to hook you. Now that you are no longer useful to the sociopaths, or they've moved on to new targets, they see no point in pretending any longer.

4. The long con

You realize that the sociopaths targeted you from the very beginning. In fact, they may have scoped you out before they even found a way to wiggle into your life. Some sociopaths are capable of plotting and calculating far in advance, and then brilliantly executing their plans. You were nothing to them but an objective.

5. It was all just amusement

Sometimes you cannot discern the sociopathic objective. They took nothing from you — not money, sex, a place to live, business connections, nothing of value. So why bother with all the games and manipulation? It makes no sense! Then you realize they were just entertaining themselves.

6. Nothing is sacred

They talk convincingly about God, religion, righteousness, spirituality, patriotism, family values, saving the planet or any other aspiration — and their behavior is the complete opposite. Their fine words are nothing but a smokescreen, lulling you into trusting them, so that they can take advantage of you.

7. Complete lack of shame, guilt and remorse

The sociopaths lie without missing a beat. They bulldoze people without blinking an eye. They even make fools of themselves without feeling foolish. They simply do not experience the emotions of shame, guilt and remorse, which, by the way, are instrumental in developing a conscience. So they have no conscience.

8. You are hurting, and the sociopaths simply don't care

The words of love or loyalty that you once heard from the sociopaths have disappeared. Now, the sociopaths are capable of incredibly cruel behavior — and then they act as if nothing happened. You are in shreds, and the sociopaths wonder what the commotion is all about.

9. Your worldview is shattered

Society tells us that we're all created equal, everyone has good inside, and we should treat others as we want to be treated. You probably took these messages to heart, and they were the rules you lived by — and they failed you when the sociopath came into your life.

Now, you've learned the hard way that these rules cannot apply to everyone. Approximately 12% to 16% of the population is disordered, and for these people you need a different set of rules — rules that are designed to protect you.

This is the most difficult part of processing your experience with the sociopath — changing your worldview. The way you understood life cannot apply to everyone you meet; some people simply are not wired like the rest of us. This is what really blows your mind — but it is also the wisdom to be gained by your experience.

Why psychopaths don't change

Lovefraud received the following question:"I've read in multiple places, written by multiple specialists, that psychopaths/sociopaths cannot be rehabilitated or changed. Surely I'm not the only person to have asked this: Why not?"

The short answer to this question is simple: Psychopaths don't change because they don't want to.

The key to any kind of behavioral change is desire. It's hard work to change the way we relate to other people, the world or even ourselves. The reason any of us embark on a self-improvement project is because we are not happy. Our relationships are not fulfilling, we believe we could do better in our careers, or we just want to feel better. For reasons like these, we are motivated to change.

Psychopaths are usually quite content with who they are. They see no reason to change.

Oh, I have heard from a few people who identify themselves as diagnosed sociopaths or psychopaths, and who have said, "It's not fun being me." But I've also heard from several who view themselves as superior to those of us burdened with pesky emotions and consciences.

For example, one person wrote to me:

> Hello my name is Alex. I would like to thank you for making your videos — they have given me an insight into how you people recognize us. WE are not to blame for your shortcomings because you are weak minded and foolish enough to be taken advantage of. We are evolutions next step — we don't allow silly emotions to cloud our judgments. In fact we use our advantage for survival because

we are natures next course. I know I sound very narcissistic and apologize for that but if you are so proud and concerned and attached to your emotions why not allow someone to make you feel like a queen for something as worldly as money? We give you what you are missing just as all of the world ecosystem has since the beginning of time. It's funny how we have been so easily classified and even now as I attempt to alter myself in order to become unparallel to descriptions of us, I find it very difficult to even perceive. I would like to boast of my strategic victories over hearts but I would fear you making another video and making this game more difficult, of course it would make it much more challenging and pleasurable when enjoying the hunt. Well you take care Donna. Bye.

Illness and personality disorders

Generally, if you have a mental illness such as anxiety, depression or post-traumatic stress disorder, there was a time before the illness began during which you were reasonably healthy. Then something happened — either an experience or biological change — that caused the illness to begin.

You know what it's like to feel better, and you want to return to the state of health.

Personality disorders are different. Most psychopaths are well on the way to disorder by adolescence, and many show signs as children, even as very young children. So there never was a time, as fully developed human beings, when they were "healthy."

Psychopaths are not loving, ethical people who go bad. They never had the capacity for love, or concern for the wellbeing of others, to begin with.

How the disorder develops

How does this happen? First of all, experts pretty much agree that there is a large genetic component to psychopathy. Children with psychopathic parents, or psychopathy somewhere on the family tree, can be born with a genetic predisposition for the disorder to develop.

Whether the disorder actually does develop may be a function of the parenting that the children receive, or the environment that they grow up in.

Unfortunately, psychopaths make lousy parents. At best, they regard the children as possessions, and care for them about as well as they care for their cars. At worst, they try to turn the children into Mini-Me's, or abuse them.

Many Lovefraud readers have realized, with trepidation, that they share children with a psychopath. There are steps these parents can take to try to prevent the disorder from developing in children, which Dr. Liane Leedom outlines in her book, *Just Like His Father?*

It's not easy. In fact, sometimes the genetic predisposition is so strong that nothing can be done to overcome it.

But if there is any chance of preventing people from becoming psychopaths, it's when they're young. That's why Lovefraud advocates keeping disordered parents out of children's lives as much as possible — to limit the effect of their bad parenting.

Drive for dominance

So how exactly does the disorder develop? Dr. Liane Leedom believes it is a result of an out-of-control drive for dominance.

We all have a drive for dominance to a certain degree — this is what makes us want to be successful, become a leader, or even drive a hot car. But in most of us, the drive for dominance is tempered by our ability to love. Because we are also concerned about the wellbeing of others, we can put the brakes on behavior that we know will hurt other people.

Psychopaths don't have an ability to love, so they don't have any brakes on their aggressive behavior.

No connection to others

What psychopaths are missing is a true feeling of connection with other people. This can start really young.

A few weeks ago Lovefraud posted a story about the results of a study showing that 5-week-old infants who preferred looking at a red ball rather than a human face may be at risk of developing callous-unemotional personality traits. These are the traits that can morph into a full psychopathic disorder.

The researchers discuss the importance of infants making eye contact — failure to make eye contact may affect the entire development of an infant's social brain. To greatly simplify the process, this may lead to an inability to respond to another person's distress, which may lead to a lack of empathy, which may lead to an inability to love, which may lead to antisocial behavior.

Even at a young age, a psychopath experiences much more satisfaction from dominating other people than from connecting with them. Every time this individual feels pleasure due to exercising power and control over others — which can start during the "terrible twos" — the drive for dominance is reinforced.

Power and control

By the time psychopaths are adults, the desire for dominance is an integral part of their identities. They like power and control. They don't particularly care if they don't have love in their lives, because they don't know what it is.

Psychopaths do not feel any distress due to their disorder, so they don't go for therapy on their own. They'll only go if dragged in by a parent or partner, or if court-ordered. And when they get there, their objective isn't changing. It's winning.

Research has shown that therapy makes psychopaths worse. Why? Because through therapy, they learn the buzzwords, and they learn more about how they're supposed to behave. They use what they learn to improve their skills at manipulation and deception.

It's possible that if psychopaths perceive controlling their antisocial behavior to be in their own self-interest, they'll do it. Criminal psychopaths, for example, may get tired of going to prison. But although they may change their behavior somewhat, it's unlikely that they will ever become loving, caring human beings.

Unfortunately, once psychopaths are adults, they will not develop a heart and a conscience. That window closed when they were young.

Sociopaths and double lives

A reporter inquired about people who live double lives. Why do they do it? Can they maintain double lives for a long time? What are the dangers?

Like most of us at Lovefraud, I have some experience with this. My ex-husband, James Montgomery, cheated with at least six different women during our 2.5-year marriage. He had a child with one of the women. Ten days after I left him, he married the mother of the child, which was the second time he committed bigamy. And of course, he took a quarter-million dollars from me—spending much of the money entertaining these other women.

Not everyone who lives a double life is a sociopath. Some people, like spies and undercover cops, are doing their jobs. But for all those people who don't have a legitimate reason for creating an alternate existence — why do they do it?

Exploitation

Sociopaths are social predators who live their lives by exploiting others. When sociopaths live double lives, the prime reason is probably because it enables them to exploit multiple people simultaneously.

This is especially true of the parasites that sponge off of their romantic partners. I've heard of many, many cases in which sociopaths, both male and female, are involved with two, three or even more romantic relationships at once, and taking from all of their partners — money, sex, cars, entertainment, whatever. Essentially the sociopaths are looking for supply, and the more sources of supply they have, the better.

Promiscuity

Another reason for double lives is the promiscuity of sociopaths. Most sociopaths have a high appetite for sex, amazing stamina, and get bored easily. Consequently, what they really want in their sex lives is variety. So they hook up with a variety of people, in a variety of places, and engage in a variety of sex acts.

Often, however, the sociopaths' sexual partners do not share these wide-ranging proclivities. But the sociopaths don't bother to tell the truth about what they're doing. The sociopaths simply pursue their sexual agendas with multiple people, but keep everyone separate. Sometimes this involves elaborate ruses and manipulation.

Thrill of the game

This leads to another point — many sociopaths simply love the game. They love getting over on people — one expert called this "duping delight."

For example, one night shortly after we were engaged, my ex-husband came to visit me. He was driving a strange car. When I asked him whose car it was, he told me an elaborate story about it belonging to a military buddy. The truth was that he had another woman staying with him for a week, and he drove her car to my house. I don't know what reason he gave her for taking her car, but whatever it was, it was unnecessary. He could have driven his own car. I believe Montgomery just wanted to take her car to visit me for the thrill of getting over on both of us.

I've heard of other cases like this. A woman brought one man that she was dating to a trade association dinner in which another man she was dating was being presented with an award. Why? For the fun of seeing one guy squirm, and the other guy clueless.

Mask of normalcy

Finally, some sociopaths hold a job, have a family, maintain a house and go to church to provide cover for their true pursuits — sex, drugs, crime and perhaps even murder. This is how some famous serial killers operated, such as Dennis Lynn Rader, the BTK killer. He worked, was a church deacon, and killed 10 people. His wife of 34 years never knew of his desire to "bind, torture and kill."

Even when they aren't killers, many sociopaths establish "normal" lives to make it easier to pursue their exploitative interests. Some sociopaths are also extremely concerned about their image. They want to keep their places in society, and having a spouse, family, job and a hot car all contribute to their status.

In answer to one of the questions at the beginning of this article, many sociopaths can, indeed, maintain the double lives for many, many years. I've heard from plenty of women who were married 10, 20, 25 years — and then were shocked to discover what their husbands were doing throughout their entire marriages.

Dangers of the double lives

Yes, I suppose some sociopaths face danger because of their double lives — but honestly, I'm not overly concerned about them.

But the dangers to unknowing partners are serious. Sociopaths bleed their partners of money to fund their extracurricular activities. As I reported in my book, *Red Flags of Love Fraud—10 signs you're dating a sociopath,* 20 percent of Lovefraud survey respondents said that their sociopathic partners infected them with sexually transmitted diseases. In the Lovefraud blog, I've reported at least two cases of men who were convicted of knowingly transmitting HIV to unknowing sex partners.

But even when partners aren't physically harmed by the double lives of sociopaths, the psychological damage of betrayal is profound. Discovery of the truth leads to two kinds of shock: The shock at the callous actions of the sociopath, and the personal shock that the partner was totally in the dark.

Recovery, for the targets, can be long and difficult. In the meantime, the sociopaths simply move on to another life.

Sociopaths say they want love, but what they really want is supply

Lovefraud recently received the following email from a reader whom we'll call "Suzette."

It's strange, my brother (who I have no doubt in my mind is a sociopath), craves being loved. He bounces from relationship to relationship, using his girlfriends. Yet when he screws up, and has his girlfriend threaten to leave him, he acts so desperate! Desperate for human connection. He tells me that he can't live without love in his life, and that he NEEDS a girlfriend by his side.

I don't understand this. He's a drug addict, and he uses his girlfriends for support — and before he had any girlfriends, he used me, and before me, he used my mother. Why does he seem to genuinely crave LOVE, if he just uses it to exploit people? He tells me he can't stand the thought of being alone, and I believe him.

I have not only seen this in my brother, but in another person resembling sociopath as well. A craving to be loved.

I believe that even if he had every material thing in the world, he would still crave being loved. Why? I thought sociopaths were unable to feel love, yet I see and read about this time and time again. This is the reason I find it difficult to dismiss him as merely a cold-hearted imitation of a person. Contrary to the evidence, he appears to have a glimmer of humanity in him — or maybe it's all just a trick?

Background about my brother: He was abused when young, has a long history of crack addiction, scammed my mother for over 40 grand, lied about having cancer, lies constantly. He IS a sociopath.

I would really appreciate a response!

Donna Andersen responds

Suzette,

Yes, your brother may very well be desperate for human connection. The key here is understanding what kind of connection sociopaths really want.

Sociopaths aren't looking for people to love. They're looking for people to exploit.

You described this yourself in your letter. Your brother uses his girlfriends. Before that he used you and your mother.

Sociopaths view other people as nothing more than patsies to give them what they want. Different patsies have different purposes.

Sociopaths may want romantic partners for money, sex, a place to live. If a sociopath actually marries the target, it may be because the partner provides an image of respectability, while the sociopath continues with cheating, drugs or other self-centered entertainment.

Sociopaths view family and friends as backups — places to crash when the romantic partners throw them out.

Sociopaths view work colleagues as people to actually do work that the sociopath will take credit for. They view employers as targets to be ripped off.

Sociopaths view strangers as walking opportunities. All the sociopath has to do is draw the person into conversation to find out what he or she has that the sociopath wants.

So yes, sociopaths are desperate for human connection. They depend on other people to give them what they want.

When "love" doesn't mean love

So why is this so confusing? Because sociopaths talk about "love."

Your brother talked about "needing love in his life." Sociopaths commonly proclaim their love to the people they've targeted as romantic partners. They say that the new partner is the "love" they've been waiting for all their lives.

Unfortunately, when sociopaths use the word "love," it doesn't have the same meaning as when the rest of us use it. After all, sociopaths don't experience love and are not capable of love. So they can't possibly know what it means.

Some sociopaths equate love with sex. So when they say, "I love you," what they really mean is, "I want to have sex with you."

Other sociopaths may be aware that they don't experience love. But they know that in order to reel in a target, they have to say the magic words, "I love you." So they say them. And it works.

When sociopaths say they want love, what they really mean is they want supply. They want someone to provide them with money, food, sex, housing, transportation, connections — whatever.

In truly despicable cases, the sociopaths simply want someone to provide them with entertainment. They hotly pursue a romantic target, proclaiming love, showering the person with attention and affection — just for the fun of later breaking the person's heart.

7 reasons why sociopaths
are hot in bed

"Best sex ever!" that's how countless Lovefraud readers have described sex with sociopaths.

People have told me that they know the sociopath is bad for them, and they need to end their involvement, but they don't want to give up the sex!

Other people have told me that they're afraid they'll never find another partner who is so sexually exciting!

I specifically asked about sex in three Lovefraud surveys. How do people who were in romantic relationships with people whom they now believe to be sociopaths rate the sex?

- In the Romantic Partner Survey (2011) 75% reported the sex was extraordinary or satisfying, at least in the beginning.
- In the Female Sociopath Survey (2014-15), 84% reported the sex was extraordinary or satisfying, at least in the beginning.
- Even in the Senior Sociopath Survey (2016), 60% reported the sex was extraordinary or satisfying, at least in the beginning. And this was sex specifically over the age of 50.

Why is this? Why are sociopaths so hot in bed? Here are seven reasons:

1. Sociopaths crave stimulation

The desire for excitement and stimulation is an integral part of the disorder. Sex, of course, is one of the most stimulating activities a human being can enjoy. Sociopaths want it. A lot.

2. Sociopaths get a lot of practice

They start young and engage frequently. Precocious sexuality is one of the early behavior problems typical of a sociopath. As they get older, sociopaths continue to engage in frequent, casual sex. Sociopaths have plenty of partners, and plenty of opportunities to learn.

3. High levels of testosterone

All sociopaths, both male and female, have very high levels of testosterone. This is the hormone that makes people compete for partners and then mate with them. So with high testosterone, sociopaths do a lot of competing and mating.

4. Lots of energy

This means endurance. In fact, many sociopaths require very little sleep. So what do they want at night instead of sleep? Sex.

5. No fear or shame

Sociopaths have no fear and no inhibitions. Consequently, they fail to develop guilt, shame, a conscience or a sense of morality. Social proscriptions against particular acts mean nothing to them. They don't care about the discomfort of their partners either.

6. Sex with anyone

Sociopaths come in many sexual orientations — straight, gay, bisexual, and all of the above. Many sociopaths are neither straight nor gay — they will have sex with anyone. In some cases, a sociopath's sexual orientation may be described as "fluid." With all the experimentation, they learn plenty of new techniques.

7. Sociopaths get bored easily

Sociopaths want sex in a lot of different ways, in a lot of different places, and with a lot of different people.

While you are their object of desire, your encounters may seem highly erotic. But sooner or later, the sociopath gets bored. Then, in search of more stimulation, the sociopath may push you to participate in activities that you find uncomfortable.

If you decline, the sociopath will most likely look for new partners — especially partners who are willing to go along with his or her desires.

The bottom line

So what does all this mean for sociopaths and sex? They have voracious appetites, they indulge often and anything goes.

But just because there's sex — even what appears to be wild, passionate sex — doesn't mean there's love. Sociopaths may be technically competent lovers, but there will never be any true intimacy or emotional sharing involved.

Why do psychopaths want to mess with your head?

Lovefraud received the following question from a curious reader:

> Why is it so important to psychopaths to get inside someone's head and "mess with them," such as gaslighting, and other head games?

This particular Lovefraud reader has endured stalking behavior from a psychopathic man for years. He has put her under surveillance, driven her from apartments, interfered with her job, and more — for no discernable reason.

They were not romantically involved. He did not take money from her. So the question is, why does he bother?

Dominance behavioral system

It's a question that goes to the core of the psychopathic disorder, and one that Dr. Liane Leedom has addressed in a scientific paper that is now being reviewed by a well-known journal.

Dr. Leedom believes psychopaths do what they do in order to satisfy their unending desire for power and control. She says that the dysfunctional behavior of psychopaths is motivated primarily by the dominance behavioral system.

This is very different from how mental health experts generally define psychopathy.

Usually, psychopaths are described as people who lack remorse or a conscience. This is certainly true, but it doesn't explain why psychopaths go out of their way to torment other people. If they have no empathy, why don't psychopaths just ignore people and leave them alone?

Pleasure from power

The answer is that psychopaths derive pleasure from having a physical, mental or emotional impact on others. They experience power and control as immensely rewarding.

Psychopaths love being the puppet master. They get a thrill out of pulling strings and making people jump.

A variation of this phenomenon is the psychopathic penchant for useless lying.

All psychopaths lie. When psychopaths are in trouble, you can understand them lying to get out of trouble. But many Lovefraud readers have noted that psychopaths lie for no reason at all.

They lie when they don't have to. They lie when they would be better off telling the truth. They lie for the fun of it.

Dr. Paul Ekman coined a term for this: "duping delight."

Convincing targets to believe something that is false is a way of exercising power and control over them. Psychopaths experience this as fun.

Evolution

Where does the dominance behavioral system come from? Dr. Leedom explains that its roots are in our evolution as a social species. Structures have developed in our brains that carry dominance impulses, and the circuitry is influenced by hormones.

So a psychopath engages in dominance behavior, hormones are released in the brain that cause feelings of pleasure, the psychopath wants to feel the pleasure again, so he or she engages in more dominance behavior. And so it goes, around and around in a vicious circle.

It is normal for people to have a power motivation. This is the motivation that makes us want to succeed, achieve and be leaders. Unfortunately, in psychopaths, the power motivation is out of control.

Criminal behavior

In some psychopaths, the drive for power and control leads to criminal behavior. They take what they want, regardless of to whom it belongs or who may be hurt.

Others, however, do not engage in behavior that is likely to have them arrested and prosecuted. It's not that they have any qualms about breaking the law. It's just that they would rather not have their lives interrupted by going to prison.

Many psychopaths, therefore, find more subtle ways to feed their need for domination. They engage in behavior that is immoral and unethical, but not necessarily illegal. They cause problems of the "he said she said" variety. They compromise their targets, so that if the targets try to seek justice, no one believes them.

By taking a more low-key approach, psychopaths can have their fun, and keep having fun.

So they engage in lying, gaslighting and manipulation. They engage in low-level harassment — aggressive enough for them to get a thrill, but not aggressive enough to incite a response from the legal system.

Psychopaths mess with your head because pulling the strings feeds their desire for power and control.

Sociopaths as chameleons — they become whatever they need to be for their latest scam

My sociopathic ex-husband, James Montgomery, considered himself to be an entrepreneur, the equal of any man who ever built a commercial empire. As he was seducing me, painting a glimmering picture of how successful and rich we would become, he proclaimed that he would be "the next Walt Disney."

When Montgomery went to business meetings, he wore a jacket, trousers, and a polo shirt. He refused to wear ties, but he always had a silk square in his jacket pocket. He told me that even when he was young, he always dressed up in jackets and cravats, eschewing the psychedelic fashions of the 60s. (For more about my story, it's all in my book, *Love Fraud*.)

So you can imagine my surprise when I heard that he'd been spotted at a train station in Katoomba, Australia, in a totally different look:

> He was wearing: red/orange pants, hippie sandals, caftan like long top to ankles in multiple colours, big round glasses with pink lenses, long scarf draped around his neck and over his shoulder nearly touching the ground and a hat which looked like a beanie. A long white beard probably about 12/15inches long and I would say weighing about 150 to 175 kilos or more. Imagine a man 6ft 2ins tall 175 kgs and wearing that get up!!!

James had tried to hook up with the woman who provided this description, while he was still dressing like an entrepreneur. She escaped. So when she saw Montgomery, her only thought was to avoid him. She later wished that she had taken his picture with her iPhone. So do I.

Changing his look

When Montgomery was spotted in the clown outfit, he was approximately 70 years old and 330 to 385 pounds. So why would a man who sneered about exotic wardrobes all his life, who never mentioned any connection with the peace-and-love ideals of the counterculture, suddenly dress like an overweight flower child?

Well, it turns out that Katoomba is known for its "artsy, hippie" lifestyle. One of the highlights of the year is the Katoomba Winter Magic Festival.

I assure you, Montgomery had no interest that type of event when I knew him. In fact, shortly after we became engaged, I went to the Philadelphia Folk Festival, which I'd attended for 20 years with a large group of friends. Although quite a few potheads in tie-died shirts roamed the campground, it was nothing like the Katoomba festival. Still, Montgomery refused to go.

So what changed? Why was he wearing round glasses with pink lenses? Necessity.

There are several hippie communes around Katoomba. I assume they were cheap places to live, and Montgomery — who promised me that we'd be living "in the lap of luxury" — was surviving on a paltry pension. He was probably living in one of the communes because it was all he could afford.

If James Montgomery were going to live in Katoomba, he needed to blend in. So he reinvented himself as a hippie.

Devalue and discard

How is this possible? How to you change from a globetrotting entrepreneur to a hippie in a flowing caftan? For a sociopath, it's as simple as changing clothes. Why? Because they are empty inside.

Sociopaths do not have character. They do not have deeply held convictions or beliefs. They do not have roots in their communities or ties with their families. They are shells of human beings, with no substance.

This is why they can walk away from any relationship, even marriages of 20 or 30 years, without a backward glance. Their only concern is what they can get from a person in the present moment. If their partner is no longer a useful source of supply — of money, support, connections, or whatever — they see no reason to hang around. It's the "devalue and discard" routine.

You may have observed the incredible lack of response when someone close to the sociopath, or close to you, dies. A sociopath may appear to be grief-stricken, but it's an act, all for show. Or, the sociopath may not even bother, saying something like, "They're gone. Get over it."

No core

Sociopaths do not have the ability to form deep connections with any person, place or ideal outside of themselves. There is no core.

Instead, sociopaths live from exploit to exploit. When their circumstances change, they adapt. If one business idea fails, they blame someone else and come up with a new one. If one romantic partner dumps them, they already have another lined up. Sometimes they're not even fazed by getting busted and going to prison — it's just a new place to run their con games.

We may have seen them proclaim head-over-heels love for us and then quickly do something to intentionally hurt us. Or, they may cry and grovel when we kick them out, and the minute we let them back, act as if nothing had happened.

They can do this because there is noting inside them. They are empty.

For those of us who can love, who can make lasting connections, it may be difficult to imagine the shallowness of this existence. So let me give you a visual. Just think of them as life-sized cardboard cut-outs of human beings. That's really all they are.

Do psychopaths
know what they are?

*L*ovefraud recently received this email from the reader who *posts as "Flicka."*

Most experts seem to say that psychotics know what/who they are — different from the rest of society. However, I question whether or not this is true. My experience has been that they SEEM to sincerely believe they are a superior group of humans, intellectually, physically, emotionally and the ultimate future of the human race. I.e., when confronted with their outright lies, accusations, priorities, misjudgments, lack of morals, compassion, they either sincerely defend their lack of emotionalism as a sign of their superiority or call you absolutely "crazy." If this response is part of their "act," they must realize they're different from the rest of us — not just mentally and emotionally superior.

What is your opinion?

Sincerely,

Flicka

P.S. In my personal case, my 5 children defend their psychotic traits with what appears to be complete sincerity.

Psychotic vs. psychopathic

First of all, I'd like to clarify the difference between "psychotic" and "psychopathic."

People suffering from psychotic disorders lose contact with reality. Here's the definition from the U.S. National Library of Medicine:

Psychotic Disorders

Psychotic disorders are severe mental disorders that cause abnormal thinking and perceptions. People with psychoses lose touch with reality. Two of the main symptoms are delusions and hallucinations. Delusions are false beliefs, such as thinking that someone is plotting against you or that the TV is sending you secret messages. Hallucinations are false perceptions, such as hearing, seeing, or feeling something that is not there.

Schizophrenia is one type of psychotic disorder. People with bipolar disorder may also have psychotic symptoms. Other problems that can cause psychosis include alcohol and some drugs, brain tumors, brain infections, and stroke.

Treatment depends on the cause of the psychosis. It might involve drugs to control symptoms and talk therapy. Hospitalization is an option for serious cases where a person might be dangerous to himself or others.

Psychopathy

Interestingly, there is no concise definition of psychopathy. Even in *Without Conscience,* the classic book by Robert Hare, Ph.D., here's the shortest description I could find:

> A self-centered, callous, and remorseless person profoundly lacking in empathy and the ability to form warm emotional relationships with others, a person who functions without the restraints of a conscience.

Dr. Hare doesn't believe anyone should be called "a psychopath." Instead, he says a person with this disorder should be described according to his or her score on the Psychopathy Checklist Revised (PCL-R), the test he developed to measure an individual's traits and symptoms.

Here's the key point: Psychopathy is not an illness; it is a personality disorder. As Dr. Hare says in *Without Conscience:*

Psychopaths are not disoriented or out of touch with reality, nor do they experience the delusions, hallucinations, or intense subjective distress that characterize most other mental disorders. Unlike psychotic individuals, psychopaths are rational and aware of what they are doing and why. Their behavior is the result of choice, freely exercised.

Awareness of the disorder

Another helpful book is *Character Disturbance,* by George K. Simon Jr., Ph.D. Dr. Simon explains how traditional views of psychology simply don't work very well in dealing with personality disorders, or as he calls them, character disorders.

Classical theories, Simon explains, regard basic human needs and emotions to be universal, and people develop psychological problems because they fear or experience their needs being thwarted. In his training, he was taught never to ask a client why he or she did something, because it would put the client on the defensive.

But in working with people who have character disorders, Simon eventually learned that they know exactly what they are doing, and why. When these people say they don't understand their own motivations, they're playing dumb.

In *Character Disturbance,* Simon writes,

> Most of the time "I don't know" doesn't really mean the disturbed character is oblivious about his actions. It almost always means something else. It can mean:
> * "I never really think about it that much."
> * "I don't like to think about it."
> * "I don't want to talk to you about it."
> * "I know very well why I did it, but I certainly don't want you to know. That would put you in a position of equal advantage over me — having my number, so to speak and I won't be able to manipulate you as easily or manage your impression of me."
> * "I hope you'll buy the notion that I'm basically a

good person whose intentions were benign. That I simply made an unwitting mistake, oblivious about the harm I caused; and that I am willing to increase my awareness with your guidance."

Knowing they are different

In answer to Flicka's question, most psychopaths likely know that they are different. Some have been professionally diagnosed, after being dragged into therapy by family members or the court. They certainly didn't go for treatment on their own, because they do not experience distress due to their disorder.

Or, even if psychopaths don't know their diagnosis, they realize that they have an innate ability to manipulate, deceive and control others. They know that other people have these pesky things called "emotions" and "conscience," which make for easy exploitation.

But psychopaths do not really understand what they lack, because they've never experienced real love or closeness. Remember, there is a very strong genetic component to psychopathy, so many of these individuals are the way they are from a very young age. It's not like psychopaths were able to love, care and act with morality, and then stopped. They never had the abilities to begin with.

You can't explain the difference between the colors red and blue to a person who has been blind since birth. Likewise, you can't explain the value of "love" and "shame" to people who have never had the capacity to experience these emotions.

Replacing a sociopath with a borderline personality disordered man

Editor's Note: Lovefraud received the following email from reader Victimcindy. Donna Andersen responds after the letter.

My first relationship, after my 18-year marriage to a sociopath, was to a borderline personality disordered (BPD) man. Do you find this common, as the disordered traits are opposite in some areas? We think we are getting something new and healthy.

Spath vs BPD: sex

My spath-ex withheld sex as power. The borderline was highly sexual. My spath-ex was charming, but lacked empathy and was emotionally unavailable. He also abused substances, was opportunistic with casual sex outside marriage and secretive.

Spath vs BPD: love

The borderline was vulnerable, overly empathetic, very emotional and had undying loyalty in a clinging way. No alcohol or drug issues. The borderline needed to be in love to feel alive.

The sociopath is incapable of bonding, or love, because their goals are exploiting outside the marriage for personal pleasure. With the borderline, the lover is the center of their world. The sociopath has incredible confidence. The borderline is insecure.

Do ex-spaths lead to borderlines?

I'm very interested to know if other readers of Love-fraud have gravitated magnetically to borderlines with a false belief that the new set of disordered traits were opposite, therefore healthier than the sociopath. Of course, there are similarities, too, but they are harder to detect because we can't connect with a sociopath, while the borderline is overly connected to the idea of love with us trying desperately not to be abandoned.

The sociopath with a secret life abandons us past the love bombing stage. The sociopath is busy exploiting and manipulating.

Spath vs BPD: when it's over

Ending the relationship with the borderline, for me, resulted in his stalking me, begging me, and love bombing. Actually I'm still not able to rid myself of the BPD — he can't take "no" or "I need space" or "it's over" for an answer.

Ending the relationship with the sociopath resulted in his discarding our family and abandoning me.

The borderline refuses to go away. I'm sort of addicted to the poems, expressions of love that convince me no one will ever love me like that again. I know better.

He also plays the sociopath card — reminding me that my ex never loved me. Black and white thinking, men with money and power are sociopaths (douche bags in his terms), and he is the good guy who never wins! Convinces me in his insecurity that anyone I go after will be a scumbag with a big wallet, unlike him.

Spath vs BPD: money

He justifies his lack of generosity. I pay for the borderline — while my ex spath showered me with gifts. Of course, his unhealthy traits are my fault — i.e., I'm a gold digger. I'm shamed should I desire anything I had from the sociopath.

I know there are things in less excessive quantities for the right reasons in healthy men. Not all men with good jobs who buy dinner and travel periodically for their partners are sociopaths. Although I've not found one yet! I'm brainwashed by the borderline, who tells me no one will ever love me like he does.

Choices

I just can't seem to be attracted to anyone without a serious personality disorder. I'm terrified to open myself to anyone and I assume anyone I like has secrets. I am very educated and well read regarding the traits. The borderline took me by surprise while I was trying to avoid the sociopathic/narcissistic traits.

Thoughts? Suggestions? Information?

Thank you for your thoughts and experiences with thousands of Lovefraud readers. I wonder how many others filled the holes made by the Spath-ex with a borderline PD. You are welcome to paraphrase and post as a letter if you desire. I'd like to see if there's a trend.

Donna Andersen responds

First, some background. Antisocial personality disorder and borderline personality disorder are related. These two, along with narcissistic personality disorder and histrionic personality disorder, are referred to as "Cluster B personality disorders" in the DSM-5 (*Diagnostic and Statistical Manual of the American Psychiatric Association,* volume 5.)

Lovefraud uses the term "sociopath" to describe people who live their lives by exploiting others. This includes people who would be clinically diagnosed as psychopathic, antisocial, narcissistic, borderline or histrionic. In reality, these disorders overlap, so it's difficult to tell one from the other.

But there are differences. A key point about borderline personality disorder is that its central feature is anxiety, which is virtually absent if someone has antisocial personality disorder.

Of all the people who are diagnosed with borderline personality disorder, about 75% are women. Many of these women suffered sexual abuse while young.

However, Dr. Liane Leedom believes that many women diagnosed with borderline personality disorder actually have antisocial personality disorder, but clinicians are often reluctant to say a female is antisocial.

Males with borderline personality disorder

Interestingly, Dr. Donald G. Dutton, in his book, *The Batterer — A psychological profile,* concludes that many men who assault their wives suffer from borderline personality disorder. Dutton writes:

> The essential defining criteria for borderline personality disorder, in order of importance, are:
> - A proclivity for intense, unstable interpersonal relationships characterized by intermittent undermining of the significant other, manipulation and masked dependence;
> - An unstable sense of self with intolerance of being alone and abandonment anxiety;
> - Intense anger, demandingness, and impulsivity, usually tied to substance abuse or promiscuity.

Many of these men were abused and shamed as children, Dutton writes. They grow up feeling they can never entirely trust others or get the security or affection they need.

It's unfortunate that these abusive men suffered as children. But if they want to recover, it's their responsibility to do it.

Women who become involved with borderline personality disordered men, initially lured by what appears to be loving attention, should not ruin their own lives by continuing to tolerate abusive behavior.

How to avoid disordered men

Here is the crux of the situation for VictimCindy. You wrote:

> I just can't seem to be attracted to anyone without a serious personality disorder. I'm terrified to open myself to anyone and I assume anyone I like has secrets. I am very educated and well read regarding the traits. The borderline took me by surprise while I was trying to avoid the sociopathic/narcissistic traits.

Replacing a sociopath with a borderline personality disordered man

The best way to avoid disordered men is not to be on the look-out for sociopathic, narcissistic, or even borderline traits, although that is important.

The best way to avoid them is to work on personal recovery.

You mention your terror at opening yourself to anyone, and your assumption that potential love interests have secrets. It's important to figure out why you feel this way.

Most likely it is because of some previous life experience or erroneous belief. Your marriage to the sociopath is certainly one of those experiences, but there may have been something before that.

Whatever happened to you to create fear and mistrust is creating the vulnerability that disordered men are so good at spotting. Whatever it is, it is still inside you, and you need to get it out.

Healing the vulnerability will enable you to trust yourself, and trust that you'll be able to sense when someone is bad news.

This, in turn, will enable you to open yourself to others. With your instincts working properly, you'll know when a man is honest and authentic, and not antisocial, narcissistic or borderline.

Sociopaths and sex:
What you need to know

Most Lovefraud readers are here because you were, or are, romantically involved with a sociopath. Usually romance leads to sex, although you may have noticed that sex with a sociopath isn't particularly romantic.

The sex may be exciting, erotic and adventurous. But if you're looking for a true connection, the "sacred conjunction," you're not going to find it with a sociopath, and here's why:

Power, control and sex

According to Dr. Liane Leedom, sociopaths want three things in life: Power, control and sex. Often, sex is simply an extension of their desire for power and control.

The most egregious cases of sex-as-power, of course, are sexual assault and rape. But there are other examples that aren't as violent or obvious.

My ex-husband, James Montgomery, liked to have sex after we argued. I later figured out that Montgomery, with his superior debating skills, usually won the arguments, and I lost. This meant that he dominated the discussion, and therefore, me, which was sexually exciting to him.

So it wasn't make-up sex. He was adding physical domination to the verbal and psychological domination of winning the argument.

Excess testosterone

All sociopaths, both male and female, have very high levels of testosterone. This is the hormone that makes people compete for partners and then mate with them. So with high testosterone, sociopaths do a lot of competing and mating.

Being in a relationship doesn't stop this. Almost all sociopaths cheat.

High testosterone is also associated with aggression and criminality. When high testosterone and a high level of sociopathy combine with deviant desires, the end result can be a very dangerous individual — a violent sexual predator.

Need for excitement

Sociopaths crave stimulation and excitement. Sex is about the most stimulating activity that a human being can experience, so they want it. A lot.

And what, exactly, do they want? Variety.

This means sociopaths like sex in a lot of different ways, in a lot of different places, and with a lot of different people.

While you are their object of desire, your encounters may seem highly erotic. But sooner or later, the sociopath gets bored. Then, in search of more stimulation, the sociopath may push you to participate in activities that you find uncomfortable.

If you decline, the sociopath will most likely look for new partners — especially partners who are willing to go along with his or her desires.

But even if you go along with the sociopath's new demands, he or she will likely still look for new partners. Sociopaths see no need to remain faithful to one person.

Eventually, when all of their past activities become boring, the sociopath may pursue the taboo.

Sex as manipulation

Sociopaths know that if they can hook you sexually, you are easier to manipulate.

Here at Lovefraud, we've written frequently about oxytocin, Nature's "love glue." Oxytocin is a neurotransmitter that makes you feel calm, trusting and content, and alleviates fear and anxiety. Oxytocin is released into your bloodstream and brain when you experience intimacy — especially sex.

So when you have sex with someone, because of the oxytocin, you bond with your partner. You become more trusting with that person, and therefore more malleable.

Oxytocin does not affect sociopaths like the rest of us. They don't bond — it's speculated that they don't have the necessary oxytocin receptors.

So what happens when you have sex with a sociopath? You bond, and the sociopath doesn't. You become more likely to comply with what the sociopath wants, whereas the sociopath just keeps pursuing his or her agenda.

Are they gay?

Several times, I've appeared on the "Straight Wives – Gay Men" radio show, hosted by Bonnie Kaye.

Bonnie has heard from thousands of women who were shocked to discover that their husbands have been sexually involved with men. The women typically come to the conclusion that their husbands are secretly gay, and afraid to live their truth.

This is certainly true in some cases. But in many, many cases, the men were simply sociopaths looking for variety in their sexual pursuits.

I've also spoken with gay men and women who realized their partners were sociopaths. Many of them observed that these partners weren't authentically gay.

The bottom line is that many sociopaths are neither straight nor gay — they will have sex with anyone.

For them, sex isn't about attraction. Sex is just another manipulation technique to further their agenda.

Sociopaths and love

The core of sociopathy is an inability to love. Sociopaths cannot experience the human connection of love, the desire to take care of the person that they love.

So what do sociopaths mean when they say, "I love you?"

Some know they are being manipulative, and are just mouthing the words to get what they want. But others equate sex with love. They think sex is love. They are essentially saying, "I want to have sex with you."

Not out of control

Given a typical sociopath's tremendous appetite for sex, and the desire for variety, you might come to the conclusion that sociopaths are out-of-control sex fiends.

Not necessarily.

Sociopaths can subjugate their sexual desires in the service of a larger agenda. For example, sociopaths are quite capable of withholding sex from their partners in order to keep them off balance.

And some Lovefraud readers have reported that their sociopathic partners aren't interested in sex. (I do have to wonder, though, if the sociopath is getting sex somewhere else.)

As I said at the beginning of this article, sociopaths want power, control and sex. But they're most interested in power and control.

12 ways sociopaths say, 'It's not my fault' — what have you heard?

One of the defining characteristics of a sociopath is that they never take responsibility for anything. Nothing is ever their fault. Any problem they face is always caused by someone else, or circumstances beyond their control.

I'll bet that a young sociopath invented the excuse, "The dog ate my homework."

Early in my relationship with my sociopathic ex-husband, James Montgomery, he explained that his innovative business venture wasn't built because "the government took his land." Of course, he never mentioned the fact that he never owned the land, and never raised the money to buy the land. He just blamed the government for his business failure.

Since I launched Lovefraud, I've heard countless stories of sociopathic excuses for their problems and antisocial behavior, like these:

- I'm screwed up because I was abused as a child.
- It's not my fault that I lost my job — the customer ticked me off.
- I'm not to blame for raping a 14-year-old — she threw herself at me.
- I quit because my boss is a moron.
- I got arrested because the cops had it in for me.
- My ex is mentally unstable — but I put up with her for years.
- My ex won't let me see my kids because she's a psycho b*tch.
- The government froze my bank accounts so I can't access my money.

- I failed because the teacher hates me.
- The guy was so hot-looking that I had to sleep with him.
- The driver gave me a dirty look, so I had to speed past him.
- The dog wouldn't stop barking so I had to kill it.

In making excuses like these, sociopaths have one or more of these related objectives:

- Playing the victim
- Blame shifting
- Gaining sympathy

They are trying to convince the target — that would be you — that they deserve to be believed, trusted or helped, because they are not responsible for whatever problems they face.

If someone who you believe may be a sociopath is making excuses, here's what you need to keep in mind:

- Sociopaths lie a lot, so any excuse may be a total fabrication.
- Even if sociopaths aren't lying, they always have an ulterior motive.
- The excuses are attempts at impression management, to convince you to give them what they want.

So what outrageous excuses have you heard from sociopaths? Add your examples to the list.

Sociopaths and love

If you're like most Lovefraud readers, you're here because you were romantically involved with a sociopath. This person probably declared love for you repeatedly, exuberantly and convincingly. Then the individual lied to you, betrayed you, cheated on you, abused you and perhaps even threatened you.

You were left stunned, distraught and devastated. How could someone who loved you treat you so badly?

A letter Lovefraud received might help you understand why that person's love was so shallow:

> I have read several articles on your site out of curiosity and boredom over the past few weeks, and I agree with almost all of their content. If I weren't a sociopath I would probably find some of those articles useful. In my opinion, however, you seem to have missed one important point about us. I'm not blaming or criticizing you for this, because it isn't your fault. This point is that we can love in some way.
>
> It isn't some intense feeling. You aren't "attached" to the other person. It is more like a different way of seeing a person. They stop being just another background character in your life, who does things for you and who you occasionally have conflicts with. Instead, you enjoy their company, feel protective and possessive of them, and become very disappointed if they die or otherwise fall out of your life. Another sociopath, a friend of mine, once told me that he felt a similar way for his girlfriend, and he was surprised that I could relate to this.
>
> What I think is strange about this version of love is that, for me at least, I had the same feeling for a close

friend who has since died, my pet guinea pig, and a boyfriend who I became bored with and broke up with. In the latter case, I felt disappointed when I realized we had nothing new to talk about, and we had fallen in to a rut. The disappointment was over by the time I formally broke up a few days later.

This particular sociopath equates "love" with "enjoyment." From her point of view, if the enjoyment is no longer in the relationship, neither is love.

Other sociopaths equate love and sex. When they say, "I love you," what they are really saying is, "I want to have sex with you."

So sociopaths may not always be lying when they say, "I love you." Sociopaths may think they do love you. They simply don't know what the word means.

Three parts to love

What exactly is love? Poets, playwrights and songwriters over the ages have struggled to describe the sensation of falling in love, and the pain of losing love. No matter how beautiful the language, words are often inadequate. We just know love when we feel it.

Scientists have also tried to explain love. Philip R. Shaver and Mario Mikulincer wrote a paper called *A Behavioral Systems Approach to Romantic Love Relationships: Attachment, Caregiving, and Sex*. Their explanation of love is useful for us because it illustrates why sociopaths can appear to be in love, when they really aren't.

Shaver and Mikulincer say there are three distinct components to romantic love:

- Attachment — you want to be around and spend time with the person you love.
- Sex — you want to have physical relations with the person you love.
- Caregiving — you want to take care of the person you love. You are concerned about his or her health, well-being and growth.

Real love has all three of these components. Sociopath, however, only experience two of them.

Sociopaths fail at caregiving

Sociopaths experience attachment — they definitely want to be with you, especially in the beginning. And they certainly want sex.

But sociopaths are not capable of true caregiving. They really are not concerned about you, your future or your fulfillment. Sometimes they seem to be taking care of you, but it's not because they actually want what is best for you. Sociopathic caregiving is all about manipulation and control.

This is why love with a sociopath is so confusing. They do actually want to be with you. The sex is often extraordinary. They sometimes pretend to take care of you. And sociopaths can keep the act going for a long time — until you are no longer useful to them, or they lose interest.

Another email

I never replied to author of the above email — there is no point in engaging a sociopath. So about a week later, she wrote again.

> At this point, I'm sure that if you were going to reply to my letter, you would have by now. Why haven't you written back? I considered writing it from the perspective of a normal person, but I figured that you would see through it if I began with, "My friend has this disorder and SHE said..." Do you think that just because I'm different from you that I deserve to be ignored? It isn't my fault that I was born a certain way. You could have just as easily been born a psycho. Would you ignore normal people because you think you're better than them? I don't. I know that both types of people — and we are both people, I hope you aren't so deep in your own world as to think we aren't — have their merits, strengths, weaknesses, and perspectives that are worth considering. Don't you agree?

Sociopaths and love

Actually I don't agree. Yes, it's sad that sociopaths are born with the genetics for the disorder, and often grow up in difficult, even abusive, environments. But when someone says she's a sociopath, and sounds like a sociopath, I have a choice on how to respond. I'll play it safe and stay away.

Sociopaths change
how we look at the world

Most of us grow up believing that all people are created equal, that human beings are basically good, and everybody wants to be loved. These are the messages we learn in school, in church, and in the age of political correctness, from the media.

These beliefs are the lenses through which we view the world and the people in it. Our beliefs influence how we perceive and understand the behavior of those we meet. And, for about 84 percent of the population, the beliefs work just fine.

Bad treatment

Then we realize that someone in our life isn't treating us well. We may think this person is reacting to our behavior, that we're doing something to provoke anger or elicit criticism — after all, that's what we're told.

We know we're not actually doing what we're accused of doing, so we try to figure out where the outbursts and hostility are coming from — did he or she have a difficult childhood? Is he or she still suffering from the pain of a former relationship?

We try to understand and accept. We stop asking questions; we stop doing things that "push buttons." But nothing changes. In fact, we're treated worse than ever.

So we take to the Internet to find out the reason for the behavior. We Google "pathological lying" or "domestic abuse" or "cheating." Or, we describe our experiences to a friend, and our friend says, "It sounds like a sociopath."

We find a checklist of sociopathic behavior, and, to our shock and dismay, it exactly describes the person who is causing us so much pain.

126

Why do they do it?

I can't tell you how many times Lovefraud readers have told me stories that follow this basic outline. When I talk to people on the phone, the question I hear most often is, "Why do they do that?"

- Why do they lie, even when they'd be better off telling the truth?
- Why do they blame me for everything?
- Why won't they let me go, when they're already seeing someone else?
- Why are they telling everyone that I'm mentally unbalanced?
- Why do they want to ruin me?

The answer to these questions is: They act this way because they're sociopaths, and that's what sociopaths do.

Shattering beliefs

Learning that sociopaths exist is like an earthquake, a tsunami, for our belief system.

Our ideas that that all people are created equal, that human beings are basically good, and that everybody wants to be loved, are not totally correct. Yes, these ideas apply to most people in the human race — but not everyone. Twelve percent to 16% of the people who live among us are fundamentally different, rotten to the core, and unable to love.

This is why experiences with sociopaths are so disorienting. Not only have we suffered physical, financial, emotional or psychological abuse, but we are also forced to accept that our entire understanding of life and other people is flawed.

This is why we feel like the rug has been pulled out from under us. This is why we feel like we cannot trust ourselves. Realizing that social predators live among us causes our worldview to collapse.

What we have learned, through painful experience, is that there are exceptions to what we previously believed. We now know

127

that there are people who look just like us and act just like us — at least when we first meet them. But their objective is not to live alongside us; instead, they want to exploit us.

We now know that sociopaths exist. With this information we can modify our worldview, realizing that we must carefully evaluate the people we let into our lives.

Overcoming the hype
to educate people about sociopaths

Lovefraud recently received the following email from a reader whom we'll call "Eleanor."

Thank you for your wonderful site Lovefraud! It has helped me tremendously. I am still with my sociopath husband, but am quietly and surely planning on leaving. We have a few children so it really makes it more complicated.

He has now gone up to the next stage in what I've read sociopaths love to do. I'm so thankful that I read about it before he did it and know how to react and what to expect! He's started to call up my family, giving them a sob story about how broken he is and how I won't get any help (we've gone through a few counselors, with no obvious results as they've all been taken in by his acting abilities).

Now my question to you is, knowing he's doing this, how can I have my close family not be influenced by him or believe him? To know it's useless to fight him — that's a given (except in court, I will do whatever I can so that he doesn't get custody of the children). But what can I say to my family to let them not take sides, realize he's lying to them, and have them not believe him? I tried to tell them this but his authentic depressed behavior got to them more. I don't want to be left alone without any support and want to catch this in the bud.

After I read your wonderful site I realize he's been doing this for years. He'll see I'm talking to a specific friend too much, and suddenly she'll stop calling. I tried hard to think if I did anything to offend her, and I didn't. Before I just had vague suspicions, but now I see clearly that he probably called her or her husband and spread lies that I told about her (I have only said good things about her, so there's nothing truthful that he could say that would be bad). This has happened with past counselors also. One I finally had the courage to call and told her what he said that she said, and she was very upset and said she never said that about me and she'll clear it up.

People don't know

The problem Eleanor faces is that people in general do not know that sociopaths exist. They do not know what sociopathic behavior looks like. So because people do not understand that there are those among us who intentionally feign distress and unhappiness, casting themselves as the victim, they do not realize that what they are witnessing is nothing but an act, and they are being conned by a sociopath.

Eleanor needs to educate her family about sociopaths, but she needs to do it carefully. If she rants and raves that they should not to believe her husband because he is a sociopath, they will probably look at her like she is nuts. In fact, her husband may already be telling them that he's very concerned about Eleanor, because she's becoming mentally unglued. The family may begin to think that the husband is right, and Eleanor does, in fact, have mental issues.

Why would they think this? Because they probably believe that sociopaths are all deranged serial killers. If Eleanor's husband hasn't killed anyone, or if he isn't violent, then she must be nuts.

Silence of the Lambs

A few days ago I watched *The Silence of the Lambs*. This is, of course, the movie that features Anthony Hopkins as Hannibal Lecter, the cannibalistic psychopath.

Even though the movie came out in 1991, I'd never seen it. I don't like horror movies or scary movies, so I never wanted to. But since we spend so much time talking about how people don't understand what a psychopath really is, I figured I needed to see the movie that created so much misinformation, so I ordered it from

Netflix. I was so apprehensive that I actually had nightmares several days before watching the film.

Two things struck me about *Silence of the Lambs*. First, Jodie Foster was really young in the movie. Second, no wonder people think psychopaths are all brilliant, cold-blooded serial killers.

The movie won five Academy Awards, including Best Actor and Best Actress for Hopkins and Foster, along with Best Picture, Best Director and Best Adapted Screenplay. The American Film Institute named Hannibal Lecter, as portrayed by Hopkins, as the number one film villain of all time.

In the beginning of the movie, the medical director of the prison where Lecter is kept says, "Oh, he's a monster. A pure psychopath. So rare to capture one alive." And Lecter does display psychopathic behavior. But his behavior is so off the charts that I don't know if there are any real-life cases as bad as he is.

Lecter is highly manipulative. The problem, however, is that his manipulation is obvious. His evil is obvious. And, of course, the guy is in prison for crimes so heinous that they put him in a straight jacket, strap him to a gurney and put a full mask on him to prevent him from literally biting someone's head off.

I can see how the image of a psychopath from *The Silence of the Lambs* could be seared into someone's brain. Unfortunately, the cartoon image of Hannibal Lecter may prevent people from identifying the real psychopaths who live among us.

After watching this movie, I feel like my decision to use the term "sociopath" on Lovefraud, instead of "psychopath," was correct. No matter how many academic papers psychology researchers publish about the behavior of psychopaths, they'll never be able to overcome the image of Anthony Hopkins ripping a cop's face open with his teeth.

Red Flags of Love Fraud

Lovefraud's goal is to educate people about sociopaths and what they're really like, especially in intimate and family relationships. Towards that end, today I am sending my second book to the printer. It's called, *Red Flags of Love Fraud — 10 signs you're dating a sociopath*. Here's the description from the back cover:

What everyone who wants a loving relationship needs to know about social predators

Charisma, charm, so much in common and sexy too— is your romantic interest a dream date, or a sociopath? Millions of these social predators live among us, and they don't look or act like serial killers. Rather, they present themselves as the love you've been waiting for all your life. *Red Flags of Love Fraud* identifies the clues and patterns of behavior that may indicate your partner is actually an exploiter. This book explains why you may be vulnerable, how the predators seduce you, how you become psychologically bonded, and how to break free of the trap.

I asked a former employee, whom I hadn't spoken with in many years, to proofread the book. It turned out that she, too, married a sociopath. She told me, "If I'd read this book 10 years ago, it would have changed my life. Literally."

My hope is that people will read the book, recognize the behaviors and realize that they're dealing with a sociopath. My bigger hope is that people will read the book, learn the warning signs, and avoid becoming involved with a sociopath in the first place.

Explaining the behavior

But back to Eleanor — she's dealing with a husband who is in full manipulation mode, trying to remove her support system by lying to her family and friends. My guess is he's also running a smear campaign, subtly disparaging Eleanor to make her less credible.

First of all, I am really glad that Eleanor had the nerve to tell one of the counselors what her husband said. I'd be interested to know how that situation plays out — does the counselor start to get what is happening? Or does she fall for the husband's lies again?

As far as the rest of her family is concerned, I think Eleanor needs to thoroughly educate herself about exactly what a sociopath is and how they behave. One way to do it is by reading Lovefraud carefully. She should learn about the key symptoms. She should even be able to quote some statistics about how many millions of sociopaths live among us.

Then, when appropriate opportunities arise with individual family members, she can present this information coolly and calmly. In fact, when her husband does something right out of the sociopathic playbook, she can explain how it is typical sociopathic behavior. For example, his sob story about how broken he is perfectly illustrates the pity play.

It's important not to get upset or angry while conveying such information, because that would create the image that Eleanor is nothing but a scorned woman. People can't listen to someone who is upset; they put up their defenses. And, presenting this information while upset could play right into the hands of the husband, who is probably saying that Eleanor is mentally unbalanced. So the best way to communicate this information is dispassionately.

Letters to Lovefraud:
I am a sociopath

Lovefraud received the following email from a man who says he is a sociopath. It is published for educational purposes, to provide insight into how he thinks. Comments will not be allowed on this post.

I'm a sociopath. I've known for a very long time that I'm a sociopath and that's that. I'm writing to you because I want your opinion. Let me tell you a bit about myself. I am a highly intelligent male with an IQ of 167. Everyone around me calls me a genius or prodigy; I just think I'm me. I am what I am and it's the only world I know. I am exceptionally good at deduction and reading people. The best example I give for myself would be Sherlock Holmes for the BBC TV series *Sherlock*. I can read a lot of things off people. Paired with my high IQ, my ruthlessness makes me elite. Let me describe my view on this.

No feelings of empathy, remorse or guilt

I don't think it's a bad thing that I don't feel empathy, remorse and guilt. I think it's a benefit, an evolved response. From what I read about empathy and guilt, I keep drawing the same conclusion: that those feelings would get in the way of my plans and schemes. They would impede on my efforts of success. We are evolutionarily built to succeed. I don't see how those emotions would help us. Why feel sorry for someone? Because they are weak? Why should we give up on our goals just because someone got in our way and got hurt. I do things sometimes that ordinary people find appalling. I don't see why it's bad.

Smarter than most people

Aren't ordinary people so boring? I get an insatiable desire for adventure and stimulation. It is so frustrating when everyone around me is so moronic. It aggravates me. If I understand something and can think of something, then WHY CAN'T YOU? I get that I'm much smarter than those around me, but still. I spend lots of time wondering what it would be like to have a slow mind, a mind that isn't acting like a freight train processing and sorting incoming information and stimuli. Sometimes I wish that I could feel emotions, just for a day. I don't think of my sociopathy as a disorder. It's a benefit. It shows that we are better than ordinary humans and are the perfect predators. Emotions seem incredibly annoying.

Attachment instead of love

As for the whole subject of sociopathy and love. I don't love people but rather I am attached to people. I care about few people, but when I do care about someone, it's a very intense attachment to that person and it's very difficult to explain how it feels. I know that boring, ordinary people don't feel like this, but I think it's rather stimulating. Why should I care about this person? Why would I do something for this person unless it benefits me? Ordinary people would describe it as selfish, but I think it's logical. I don't love these people, but I am very protective of them. If someone crosses a person that I care about, I will talk to them for 5 minutes and immediately know their weaknesses. I will then exploit these weaknesses to psychologically rip them apart.

It is in some way fun to have to blend in with ordinary people. All the friends, relationships, classes and conversations are just forms of camouflage. It's satisfying to remain hidden but I will admit that sometimes it's exhausting, having to put on different masks. That's why I self-identified myself as a sociopath to someone I know as an experiment, and admittedly so I could talk to an ordinary person about myself. What's the point of doing great things if you don't get to share the stories of your success with people every now and again?

I find it excruciatingly boring to talk to ordinary people sometimes. "Look at me. Look at all my problems. I need help. Blah blah blah." I don't give a f**k. Some particular people's problems do elicit a sort of challenge or opportunity, which I can't help but investigate. These sorts of things interest and attract me. I have a gut feeling that one day I'll unwittingly walk into a trap set by some of the ignorant idiots in the world who are out to get us because they feel we are "abominations" and "creatures," but until then I will enjoy my subjects thoroughly.

Meeting other sociopaths

It's delightfully interesting to meet another sociopath. I've only have the fortune to meet another sociopath once and I enjoyed every minute of it. I got to study the exterior of a sociopath, as did he. I didn't have to test him, as I could spot him immediately. I actually wondered for a moment how everybody else didn't realise what he was but then discarded that thought, because due to my natural "talent" I can easily discern things about people. I can read between the lines. Now tell me, how can I change this? Because apparently it's a bad thing. People with my so-called "disorder" have been described as "heartless monsters who leave nothing but destruction and misery in their path."

So you now have first-hand information from a sociopath. I want you to tell me, is my life all that bad? Or will it be an endless search for amusement and games? If you read this and decide that I have a problem and I need help then I promise I will go straight to therapy.

10 things sociopaths want
(besides money)

A Lovefraud reader recently asked the following important question:

> If the sociopath is not in it for money (he pays for everything with no access to my accounts) then what are other reasons to stay in a relationship if he doesn't live with me nor do we share anything financially? Many of the posts I have read involve financial fraud.

If a sociopath has targeted you, it's because you have something that he or she wants. Often it's money, but not always. Here are 10 more things that the sociopath may want:

1. Sex

Sociopaths crave stimulation, and sex is highly stimulating, so they pursue it. However, sociopaths are not slaves to their physical urges. They often use sex primarily as a tool of manipulation to get something else that they want.

2. Services

Sociopaths may want you to do something for them that they don't want to do for themselves, such as cooking, cleaning and taking care of children.

3. Housing

Even if sociopaths don't directly ask for money, they may suggest living together. They may say it's because they love you, when, in fact, they have no place to go.

4. Entertainment

Perhaps you're part of an exciting social scene. The sociopath may want to be with you just to gain access to the people you know.

5. Status

Hanging out with you may be good for their image, especially if you're rich, famous, successful or competent. Your status boosts their status.

6. Image

Perhaps the sociopath needs a partner like you to complete the image that he or she wants to present to the company or community.

7. Cover

Your presence may help them get away with a hidden agenda. You may be providing cover for the sociopath to pursue a double life of sex, drugs or crime.

8. Connections

Sociopaths may use you, your skills and your connections in order to pursue their grandiose dreams or entrepreneurial plans.

9. Duping delight

Sociopaths enjoy getting over on people — this is called "duping delight." They often manipulate, deceive and use people just for the fun of it. Some will seduce targets just so they can break their hearts.

10. Domination

Sociopaths feed on power and control, so they sometimes pursue domination for its own sake. They want to prove themselves to be more powerful than you, perhaps even powerful enough to destroy you.

If a sociopath targets you, it's because he or she sees you as useful in some way. Once you are no longer useful, you'll be dumped.

Hastening the demise of sociopaths

Millions of sociopaths roam the planet. They inhabit all segments of the population. They are male, female, rich, poor, old, young, all races, all religions, all education levels, all demographic groups. Most of them are not in prison, so they move freely among us, living their lives by exploiting others.

Many take pride in their ability to manipulate others. Some who are criminals view crime as fun. They see nothing wrong with their behavior. As long as they keep succeeding, sociopaths will continue to behave the way they do.

So how do we make them fail?

Sociopaths only want to win, so failure is losing. Failure is not being able to exploit others, or at least not being able to get away with exploiting others.

I see four steps to shutting them down, and they all revolve around education.

1. Educating the public about sociopaths

This is the first step. So many Lovefraud readers who have tangled with sociopaths have told me, "I didn't know these people existed!" Yes, they exist. Sociopaths live among us. And they are dangerous to our mental, emotional, psychological, financial, sexual and physical health.

This is why I launched Lovefraud. This is why I'm embarking on the Lovefraud High School Education Program to teach high school and college students about sociopaths. (If you're in a position to bring the program to your school, please contact terry@anderlypublishing.com.) And there are so many more people who need to be educated, including therapists, lawyers and judges. We all need to know the warning signs of sociopathic behavior, so that if we see them, we can respond appropriately—especially by running away.

2. Exposing known sociopaths

This, I believe, is the only strategy that really works against sociopaths. We can't count on winning judgments against them and actually collecting our money. We can't count on them being prosecuted or locked up. Sometimes the only way to keep them from harming others is to blow their cover.

We do need to be cautious about this, as I explained in a previous article, *Exposing the sociopath*. Many of you may not be able to skewer your exes publicly, as I did with James Montgomery. But you may be able to quietly speak your truth in your community, profession, church or wherever you know the predator is trolling for new victims. In the future, a few words of warning, coupled with growing public awareness of the disorder, may be enough.

3. Stop breeding sociopaths

Sociopaths are hard-wired for sex. They have a lot of sexual magnetism, and many Lovefraud readers have said that sex with the sociopath was the best they've ever had. But a consequence of sex, of course, is children. And because sociopathy is a highly genetic disorder, children born of sociopaths are at risk of inheriting a predisposition for the disorder.

One of the big things I hope will be accomplished through the Lovefraud High School Education program is to help young people understand that romantic relationships with sociopaths lead to nothing but trouble. If more people refuse to get involved with sociopaths, that will mean fewer at-risk children.

4. Appropriate parenting for at-risk children

Although sociopathy is highly genetic, inheriting the genes doesn't necessarily mean that every at-risk child will grow up to be a sociopath. It is the interaction of genetics and the environment, including parenting, which actually creates the disordered individuals.

Many people realize, after a child is conceived or born, that their partner is a sociopath. If this is you, you need to take steps to raise the child so that he or she does not develop this disorder. I realize that this is immensely difficult and complicated, especially when the sociopathic parent will not let go of the child, which is often the case. But the healthy parents should try, as best they can, to teach the child how to love and feel empathy. (For information on how to do this, read *Just Like His Father?* by Dr. Liane Leedom.)

Perhaps with education, perseverance and time, our descendants will see the end of sociopathy. And they'll thank us for taking the first steps to hasten the demise.

Sociopaths keep the charade going for a while

I was with my sociopathic ex-husband, James Montgomery, for two and a half years. During this time, I knew he was costing me money, but he attributed his lack of business success to "being ahead of his time." I eventually discovered that he was lying and cheating on me. But although I saw eruptions of anger, my ex was never abusive towards me—nothing like the abuse many of you have endured.

Some sociopaths can treat people reasonably well for an extended period of time, if it suits their purpose. For example, Lovefraud received the following email from a reader:

> I was not in a disastrous relationship with my S. Our relationship was less than three years, our marriage less than two, when he openly cheated and decided to leave me, then played games of false reconciliation, which in hindsight were so he could have two sex partners.
>
> The short end of my question is... How do you reconcile the basically happy marriage, the illusion of a man you married, with the horrible monster he has become in trying to create turmoil in your life and use your greatest love (your child) to hurt you?

Expressions of love

I'll get to this reader's question shortly. But first I want to review some of the information Lovefraud learned in our survey about people involved with individuals who exhibited sociopathic traits. One of the objectives of that survey was to investigate whether and how often sociopaths expressed love.

We asked the question, "Did the individual you were involved with verbally express love or caring to you?"

A total of 85% of all survey respondents said yes. And, when the individuals being described were the spouses or romantic partners of the survey respondents, rather than parents, children or others, 92% of the males and 95% of the females expressed love verbally.

How often did this happen? A total of 44% of survey respondents said the sociopathic individual expressed love daily.

Complete change

The survey also asked the following: "Please provide a brief description of the way the person you were involved with expressed love. How did this change over the course of your relationship?"

Now I've been hearing all kinds of stories about the games sociopaths play in relationships for more than five years. Yet some of the answers to this question still made my jaw drop.

A small group of survey respondents reported a complete change of behavior the moment they were committed to the relationship—moved in, married or pregnant. This startling change was reported in reference to 7% of the females and 5% of the males. Here are some of the quotes:

> *"Initially with dates, flowers, gifts and little thoughtfullness's. After I married him, he said, on the Honeymoon, 'I can stop acting now.' I thought that he was joking. I later learned he did not do jokes."*

> *"From very loving to cold indifference...started right after we were married — The change was startling — cold, distant, indifferent, condescending, mean spirited, accusatory, self righteous, irresponsible."*

> *"It changed the minute we got married. Then he owned me you see, I was nothing to him after he lured me in! All he wanted was MONEY!"*

"In the beginning of the relationship (before marriage) he was loving, caring, could not do enough for me. Called me his soul mate, his true companion in life. This continued until the day I married him, within hours after the wedding ceremony his personality shifted. It was as if I had dated and fell in love with one person, but married someone I was completely unfamiliar with, he was a stranger to me in all ways."

Doesn't exist

So, back to our reader's question, "How do you reconcile the basically happy marriage with the horrible monster he has become?"

The man this reader saw during the happy part of the marriage did not exist. It was an act, a charade, a mirage that the sociopath kept going until it no longer served his purpose. The real man is the horrible monster.

Sociopaths explain their own words

Sociopaths have no empathy. They do not feel connections to other human beings. We are mere pawns in their games. They view the world as predators and prey — they are the predators, everyone else is prey.

We ask, "How can this be?"

We object, "He said he loved me!" ("She said she loved me!")

We argue, "I said I was leaving and he cried! He begged me to stay! He said he couldn't live without me!" (The female sociopath did too.)

Well, let's take a look at what their words really mean. A Lovefraud reader visited a website frequented by sociopaths. "They had a discussion going on things they said but what they actually meant to them," she wrote.

Here's what our reader sent:

The Cheat-Sheet for What a Sociopath Really Means

1. I love you: I am fond of your companionship and put you above most, but never above me. Consider it an honor.
2. I'm sorry, forgive me: I really do not enjoy the fact that your mood has altered. Please revert back to normal.
3. I'd do anything for you: I'd do plenty to keep you right where I want you to be.
4. My condolences for your loss: *crickets* ... It's just a body. See you later when you aren't being an emotional train-wreck.

5. S/he fills my heart with joy: I haven't had this much fun playing in a long time, and the sex is more than acceptable.

6. I love my family: They're mine.

7. That's simply shocking: You've touched my morbid bone. No need to stop now...

8. Deep down, I feel I'm a good person: I'm not in prison and I stopped abusing animals, mostly. What more can you possibly demand of me?

9. I'm not a monster, I'm a human too: I'm trying to seem human, give me a break. It's not like this is particularly natural for me.

10. I have feelings too: I feel frustrated when your feelings get in my way.

11. I wouldn't lie to you: I lie to you every time I say I wouldn't lie to you.

12. I understand/respect your feelings: I appreciate your feelings because I use them to manipulate you.

13. I never meant to hurt you: mission accomplished.

14. I want to work things out: I want to work things out for today.

15. I'll always be there for you: I'll try to as long as I need something from you

Remember this: Never evaluate the words or actions of a sociopath based on what you mean by your words and actions. For a sociopath, it's all about manipulation.

Why do psychopaths lie?

All psychopaths lie. They tell big lies, small lies, outrageous lies. They lie when they would be better off telling the truth.

So why do psychopaths lie?

When normal people lie, it's generally to escape blame for a failure or shortcoming (as in, "The light was yellow"), or to preserve social dignity, (as in, "No, those jeans don't make you look fat").

In contrast, psychopaths lie in order to exert power and control over others.

Sometimes they have an agenda, such as trying to con you out of money. Once we realize that psychopaths have been lying to take things from us, we are outraged, but we can understand the purpose of the lies.

What is truly mystifying are the lies for no apparent reason. For example, I know of several cases in which psychopaths met someone online, showered them with attention, promised them the world, proclaimed their love, and when the targets finally fell head-over-heels, dumped them.

The psychopaths didn't get any money. They didn't even get any sex. So why did they go to all the trouble of seducing the targets?

For the thrill of exerting control over them.

This is called "duping delight." Psychopaths literally feel a rush when they convince people to believe their lies.

Why lying is so easy for psychopaths

Psychopaths lie like they breathe. So why does lying come so easily to them? The answer is in some of the other traits of the disorder.

First of all, psychopaths feel entitled to get anything they want, when they want it and how they want it. If whatever they want is not quickly forthcoming, they feel entitled to use any means necessary to take it. Often, the easiest and most direct approach is lying.

Second, psychopaths do not have a conscience and have no sense of moral responsibility. Because they don't feel the internal prohibitions the rest of us do, lying is easy.

Difficult to detect lies

This is why psychopaths can pass polygraph tests. A polygraph works by detecting autonomic reactions — changes in the body that are not easily controlled by the conscious mind, like heart rate and blood pressure. The basic idea is that someone who is lying will feel fear about it.

Guess what? Psychopaths usually don't feel fear, especially fear of lying. So they don't exhibit the short-term stress response that the polygraph is designed to detect.

Of course, you probably won't have access to a polygraph during your regular conversations with a psychopath. So are there any "tells" that will indicate when he or she is lying?

Tips for spotting liars

If you look online, you'll find articles like this one: *10 ways to catch a liar,* on WebMD.com. Here are the tips from that article, and my opinion of their effectiveness with psychopaths.

Tip No. 1: Inconsistencies
Yes, psychopaths are inconsistent — and they always have a reasonable explanation for the inconsistency.

Tip No. 2: Ask the unexpected
This might work for an instant — until the psychopath comes up with a plausible story, or accuses you of being paranoid.

Tip No. 3: Gauge against a baseline
The idea of this tip is to notice changes in behavior. It will

never work, because a psychopath's behavior is always erratic, so there are no changes to notice.

Tip No. 4: Look for insincere emotions

Psychopaths are experts at appearing to express sincere emotions. You may eventually catch on that they are faking it, but it will take a while.

Tip No. 5: Pay attention to gut reactions

Yes! This one is important. Your instincts or intuition will tell you something is wrong. You may not know what it is, but if you get a gut reaction, pay attention!

Tip No. 6: Watch for microexpressions

This is the basis of the TV show *Lie to Me*. I'm not sure if it works with psychopaths or not. What do you think?

Tip No. 7: Look for contradictions

It's quite possible that you'll see a contradiction with a psychopath. But the reason may not be that the psychopath is lying — it may be the result of other traits, like shallow emotions.

For example, a psychopath may say, "I stabbed the guy" with the same emotion that you would show in saying, "I sliced an apple." The psychopath may very well be telling the truth — but the words don't affect him.

Tip No. 8: A sense of unease

This means you'll supposedly notice a sense of unease in an individual who is lying. Ha! Not if the person is a psychopath.

Tip No. 9: Too much detail

Yes, a psychopath may tell elaborate stories. But the psychopath may always tell elaborate stories. So you may be used to it — and only much later realize that the stories were all lies.

Tip No. 10: Don't ignore the truth

Psychopaths are experts at mixing lies with the truth. You'll know some parts are true, and because of that, assume the rest is true. Except it isn't.

The bottom line

- All psychopaths lie.
- Psychopaths lie in order to exert power and control over others.
- Techniques for uncovering lies may not work with them.
- Your body, instincts and intuition do not lie. If you get a bad feeling about what someone is saying to you, that is your best chance of spotting the lie.

Letter from a sociopath

From time to time, Lovefraud receives email from people who identify themselves as sociopaths. Here's one that came in recently:

I have read your website, and i am not impressed. You give the impression that all sociopaths are murderers and haters, incapable of loving, and should be thrown away as a tragedy to the human race. You do not mention the difference between a high-functioning sociopath and a low-functioning sociopath. I happen to be a high-functioning sociopath, and your website is all lies and misguided information, and whats worse, you gain money out of creating a stigma of us, and abusing the victims of certain relationships, which although do happen, aren't generally what high functioning sociopaths are about. Who's the one with no conscience? I would say you.

I have no emotion, i use logic to understand what is happening. I mimic emotions of others because i know that it is important to my survival that i display emotion or otherwise people become scared. Is that really so bad? Yes, perhaps i play mind games with people because i grow so bored, but that doesn't really harm them does it? People get over it. I don't go out murdering puppies and kittens, and laugh like a comic villain. I may have mistreated some animals, but never with the intent of doing so. I may have hurt some people, but they get over it. I'm the one who has to pay for their hurt, they threaten my survival when they retaliate. I flirt with people a lot, but so do a lot of people, not just sociopaths. I do have some emotion, even if it is limited. I can pretend to have an emotion to convince myself. I act simply to feel.

You 'empaths' only have emotions so that you are scared of us, when all we are is bored, and confused harmless cheeky rascals. And to point out, adult sociopaths usually stop being sociopaths after the age of 30, so its not 'incurable' as soon as they become an adult. You try living in a world that is black and white, where any emotion has to be forced, and you have to copy others expression, and you're always so very bored, because i am, so bored. You can't blame us for needing some excitement, to survive we must have a way out of our boredom. You know nothing about what you say. We have a soul, we just can't access it as easily as everyone else.

Born with the genes

The person who wrote this letter, I was able to determine, is an attractive young woman. I'll ignore her mischaracterizations of Lovefraud — we are obviously well aware that sociopaths are not all murderers, because most of us were involved with sociopaths who didn't kill anyone. Beyond that, her letter provides a good insight into the reality of sociopaths, with all their rationalizations and excuses.

Even so, I do feel sorry for them.

Sociopathy is highly genetic, and no sociopaths asked to be born they way they are. No sociopaths asked for manipulative parents or uncaring home environments that pushed them further along the path towards disorder. That's the hand they were dealt, and it's truly sad.

Even sadder is the fact that they don't know it's sad. It's like someone born blind, who doesn't comprehend vision. Or someone born deaf, who can't understand what music may be. They were born with a limited or nonexistent ability to love, and whatever love they did have was probably snuffed out by their own disordered parents. Instead, they have an overactive appetite for power and control.

Like this young woman, sociopaths are aware that they are different. But most of them don't care. In fact, they take pride in their ability to exercise power, and look down on the rest of us. We are merely marks to be exploited.

Lessen the disorder

This young woman also said that people stop being sociopaths at the age of 30. There is no scientific evidence that sociopathy can be cured. The best we can usually hope for is that sociopaths will decide to comply with the mores of society, if only because it's in their own self-interest. They do have the power to decide that following the rules is more convenient and causes them less aggravation than violating them.

Can sociopaths actually lessen their disorder? Dr. Liane Leedom is hopeful, although she recognizes that it is extremely difficult. The fact is that many brain characteristics and functions contribute to sociopathy, and the human brain is not static. Beliefs and behaviors can cause chemical and structural changes in the brain. So if sociopaths were really committed to changing their ideas, and engaged in activities that fostered empathy, their brain structures could change. An individual willing to attempt this would probably have a lesser degree of disorder to begin with, so maybe he or she would already have seeds of caring buried within, seeds that could grow into a degree of empathy.

Inaccessible soul

I was struck by the last sentence of the letter:

> We have a soul, we just can't access it as easily as everyone else.

I actually think that the young woman is right about this. The souls of sociopaths are buried under so much negativity—anger, hatred, aggression, coldness, envy and the desire for power—that the souls can't be felt.

I don't think those of us who have been damaged by sociopaths should attempt to help them. Our first duty is to ourselves, to our own health and recovery. But I believe that we're all connected, and maybe in whatever communication we may have with a higher power, we can pray for them. It might take a long time, but maybe it will do some good.

Even if we don't see any improvement in particular individuals, praying will help ourselves. Bitterness only prolongs our own misery and harms our own health. Perhaps offering prayers, from a safe distance, will make a difference all the way around.

The Marriage Masks: Three types of sociopathic relationships

Here at Lovefraud, we've heard thousands of horror stories of marriages to sociopaths. Thinking about these unfortunate involvements, it seems to me that there are three types of romantic relationships with sociopaths. I call them the Marriage Masks, and they are:

1. Calculated exploitation

The sociopath targets an individual for the explicit purpose of exploiting him or her, using the unsuspecting partner for money, sex, a place to live or something else that the sociopath wants.

My ex-husband, James Montgomery, targeted me because I had what he wanted: money, good credit, my own home and business connections in the city where he decided he was going to make a fortune. He sweet talked me, married me and drained me, and then he moved on without a thought.

2. Passing entertainment

The sociopath finds the partner to be a suitable involvement for the present—until the sociopath gets bored, antsy, or some other individual catches his or her eye. At this point, the partner is discarded.

Mary Jo Buttafuoco described her husband, Joey Buttafuoco, in her book, *Getting It Through My Thick Skull*. To me, it seems that Joey Buttafuoco was one of those sociopaths who was simply looking for a good time, for entertainment. He worked and she was a stay-at-home mom, so he wasn't using her financially. But eventually he had an affair with a teenager, then visits to hookers, then a new wife. Changing women was like changing the scenery.

3. Image creation

In order to secure a coveted place in society, the sociopath may seem devoted to his or her spouse or family in public, but life at home, behind closed doors, is another matter entirely.

Here's an example that was recently in the news. Stephen Green, founder of a fundamentalist organization in the United Kingdom called Christian Voice, preaches against homosexuality, abortion, Islam and Jerry Springer. "The enemies of God are having their say," proclaims the organization's website. "It's time to hear the Christian Voice!"

Green portrays himself as the guardian of morality in the U.K. However, Caroline Green, his former wife, paints a totally different picture—domestic violence. The whole revolting story appeared in the Daily Mail: *In public he rails against immorality as the voice of Christian Britain, but in private he is a wife beater, says his former partner.*

> 'He told me he'd make a piece of wood into a sort of witch's broom and hit me with it, which he did,' she recalls, her voice tentative and quiet. 'He hit me until I bled. I was terrified. I can still remember the pain.
>
> 'Stephen listed my misdemeanours: I was disrespectful and disobedient; I wasn't loving or submissive enough and I was undermining him. He also said I wasn't giving him his conjugal rights.'

Missing: Ability to love

These categories are not hard and fast, and some sociopathic relationships and marriages may show signs of two or all three types. But however the dysfunction manifests, the root problem is that sociopaths are not capable of feeling real love.

They are, however, capable of acting like they feel love—at least in the beginning of a relationship. I call it the luring stage— the period of time when sociopaths do everything you'd ever dream that smitten partners would do. They call, they want to be with you, they give gifts, they make you feel cherished. They do this until they hook you.

Then, sociopathic behavior starts to reflect the real agenda—calculated exploitation, passing entertainment or image creation. The change may be subtle or sudden. The relationship may gradually devolve, it may swing back and forth between normal and unconscionable, or it may suddenly evaporate.

But at some point, the Marriage Mask slips, and we come face to face with the truth: We are being used.

Do sociopaths know what they are?

I receive a lot of email from readers, and over the years many have asked some variation of the question: Do sociopaths know what they are? Do they realize that something is wrong with them?

The answer varies with the individual sociopath, because they aren't all the same. Generally, though, I believe sociopaths know that they are different from the rest of the human race. However, most are not bothered by their difference. They view themselves as superior.

It's easy to see where this attitude comes from. Because sociopathy is highly genetic, and is influenced by the early childhood environment, sociopaths never were anything but sociopaths. They never experienced a true empathetic connection with another human being. They did not develop a desire to love and be loved. Therefore, they do not know what they are missing.

Talking to sociopaths about love and empathy is like talking to someone who has been blind since birth about the color blue. They simply have no frame of reference.

Sociopaths have totally different motivations from the rest of us. As I explained in *Sociopathic deceit: Plan or second nature?*, they are driven by the desire for power, control and winning. Because they become so good at manipulating others to get what they want, sociopaths perceive themselves as successful, and therefore superior.

When they are diagnosed

Here's a key point: Sociopaths do not feel any distress due to their disorder. (It's everyone around them, who have been deceived, manipulated, cheated on, stolen from, etc., who feel distress.) Therefore, sociopaths feel no motivation to change, and do

158

not seek treatment on their own.

When a sociopath ends up in a therapist's office, it is because he or she was forced to go there. The sociopath was dragged in by a parent or spouse, court-ordered for an evaluation, or was incarcerated and diagnosed by prison staff.

Therefore, sociopaths may be aware of their diagnosis. Again, this does not cause them distress. They either deny it, or figure out a way to use the information to their advantage.

Lovefraud published an article back in 2007 by Dr. Steve entitled, *What does the psychopath 'do' with this diagnosis?* The article makes the point that psychopaths (the term Dr. Steve uses) don't see themselves as having a problem. One of the most interesting things about this article was that it drew comments from someone with the user name "Secret Monster." He said he was diagnosed as a sociopath and had been in therapy. His comments gave a good insight into how a person with this disorder thinks.

In their own words

Lovefraud has heard from other people who identified themselves sociopaths. I've posted a few of their emails. My objective wasn't to give them a platform; it was to show Lovefraud readers how sociopaths look at the world and how they go about manipulating others. The more we understand what they're about, the better we can protect ourselves.

About a month after I posted a letter from a sociopath, I received another email from the man who wrote it:

> I was very disappointed to find that you didn't permit commenting on my letter that you posted, I was really looking forward to the responses I would receive.
>
> I decided to search my letter online and I quickly found that it spread to numerous sites. Some of the websites allowed readers to comment and this is what I mainly gathered from the comments. People found that I was arrogant and that I enjoyed "bragging" about my intellectual ability, mainly my IQ. People also made it clear that they feel sorry for me. F**k them.

Many readers shared that they know me but they don't so I assume that I represent a certain sociopathic person in their lives. An archetype of what they collectively despise.

I decided to read a couple of articles on your website which you had personally wrote and you don't have to have an aptitude at discerning to realise that you hate me. And by "me" I mean sociopaths as a whole. You do love to quote our good friends Robert Hare and Martha Stout, who are both idiots I must add.

I've been reading up, hitting the books ya know?, and I've found that some researchers and psychologists have a theory that Sociopathy/Psychopathy is not a disorder but rather an evolutionary response. Humans were created to excel and we wouldn't be that good at it if we felt bad about our achievements.

Some people are just so stupid. They cling to their moronic convictions and when confronted with contrary evidence they still hold on to their prior beliefs. It's pathetic. They say things that are blatantly false such as how all sociopaths are criminals or that the good ol' anti-sociopath people are smarter than the sociopaths. Of course there are some examples when this is true but on the most part we are smarter.

I understand that it is your hobby or maybe even job, but you do seem to dislike sociopaths. I could probably find the reason if I cared enough to read your bio that you probably have on the website but where's the fun in that? You are extremely negative towards people who you say are "struggling" with this "disorder." Seems quite hypocritical of you to go extremely anti-sociopath. You may not know it but you are breeding the next generation of sociopath haters. Of course we don't really care but I'd appreciate it if your website was more about raising awareness and helping people get over traumas than going on the full attack.

Proof of my point

I've received similar letters from a few other people who claim to be sociopaths. They say I don't know what I'm talking about, I'm judgmental, I shouldn't refer to sociopaths as if they are all monsters.

I look at these letters as typical sociopathic trivializing, blaming, manipulation—and proof of my point. Many sociopaths know exactly what they are and what they are doing. They know the difference between right and wrong. They know that they hurt people. But they are fine with their behavior and have no motivation to change.

So to answer the original question, yes, many sociopath know what they are, but they don't think anything is wrong with them.

How disordered motivation explains psychopathic behavior

Why do they do it? If you've ever tangled with a psychopath, you've certainly asked yourself that question. Why do psychopaths engage in harmful and destructive behavior?

Most psychopathy researchers explain the nasty behavior of these disordered individuals in terms of deficits. They say that because psychopaths lack empathy and impulse control, they engage in antisocial behavior.

To Lovefraud author Dr. Liane Leedom, this makes no sense — it implies that if it weren't for empathy and impulse control, everybody would be a psychopath. Deficits don't cause behavior, she says. Motivation causes behavior.

In a chapter that she recently wrote for the book *Psychopathy - New Updates On an Old Phenomenon,* Dr. Leedom argues that human motivational systems are affected by psychopathy, and that's what causes antisocial behavior.

All animals, including humans, have behavioral systems that are designed to achieve certain goals, such as survival and reproduction. These behavioral systems are rooted deeply in our biology and are reinforced through our brain reward systems.

Human beings, Dr. Leedom explains, have four social behavioral systems, and they're all seriously affected by psychopathy.

Attachment Behavioral System

Most humans seek proximity to, and bonding with, certain special individuals, such as parents and romantic partners. This is called attachment. Many researchers say it is the attachment system that is dysfunctional in psychopaths, that they are incapable of forming long-term social ties.

Research, including Lovefraud's research, indicates that this is not true — psychopaths can indeed form social ties, especially when they want to use people to provide their material needs. However, psychopaths do not form psychological and emotional bonds with others.

Caregiving Behavioral System

Most people feel a desire to take care of the individuals with whom they bond. Empathy is critical for caregiving, but empathy is impaired in psychopaths. Dr. Leedom says there is strong evidence that the caregiving system in psychopaths is deficient.

Dr. Leedom notes that antisocial mothers were found to show a lack of warmth towards their children, along with harsh and abusive discipline, passivity and neglect. Disordered fathers psychologically abused their children, even if they didn't physically abuse them. "Given all the deficits in the caregiving system, it is remarkable that psychopathic persons function as parents at all," Dr. Leedom writes.

Sexual Behavioral System

Psychopaths usually are highly active sexually, but the experience for them is also highly impersonal. Researchers have found early, frequent and coercive sex is strongly associated with psychopathy. Promiscuous sex is actually a symptom of psychopathy.

Dominance Behavioral System

In the long history of the human race, the dominance drive provided people with motivation to compete for the control of resources. In psychopaths, this drive has morphed into a power motivation.

"Dominance behavior is diagnostic of psychopathy," Dr. Leedom writes. "Glibness and superficial charm, grandiose sense of self-worth, pathological lying, and cunning/manipulative behavior comprise a dominance style that is typical of psychopathy."

Motivational theory

Dr. Leedom says psychopaths do form attachments, but they

connect with other people in order to meet their material and psychological needs.

When psychopaths engage in antisocial behavior, it is because of their excessive and aberrant dominance responses, an absent or highly disordered caregiving system, and a sexual system in which they do not bond with their partners.

In the end, Dr. Leedom says, it's not psychopathic deficiencies, but their skewed motivations, that cause their destructive behavior.

To read Dr. Leedom's full paper, look for *Psychopathy: A Behavioral Systems Approach*, on IntechOpen.com

The philosophy of a sociopath

Lovefraud received a letter from a woman whom we'll call Valerie. She met her husband, whom we'll call Dylan, at age 18, and has been with him for seven years. She thought they were happy together in their wonderful home with their family of pets.

Suddenly Dylan started acting erratically. He said he didn't want to be with Valerie any more. He picked fights. She asked Dylan to leave, but made it clear that she was willing to do whatever was necessary to help him. So he left, and wouldn't tell her where he was. Eventually, Valerie's intuition told her to check her husband's Facebook page, where she found Dylan's love letters to another woman.

Then Valerie found how Dylan described himself on another website. Here's what he wrote:

> My name is Dylan and I believe in Chaos, destruction and murder. I will contradict myself but I don't think that should make me a hypocrite. I hone my strengths and hide my weaknesses because only the strong will survive. I lie, cheat and steal. But only if it's the most intelligent plan of action; & only the stupid get caught. I'm fighting a personal rebellion I can't justify. I'm losing my mind, my friends and my morals with each passing day, but each day I pass leads me closer to finding myself. I would rather live my life in surrender to temptation than to deny my natural instincts. I never hurt those who do not hurt me first, I don't believe in physical confrontation but as in eastern philosophy I am trained to engage in it, if for nothing more than the practice of strengthening the bond between mind and body.

I know who I am, but not where I am, or why I am here. I find Art to be the only voice of reason in a place otherwise inhabited by counter-production. I promote sex, but lack emotion, I hate addicts but I believe in drugs, I make music but I destroy everything else. I bore easily but I am doomed to repeat myself.

My name is Dylan and this is only the beginning.

Whoa! Did this guy just write the sociopath manifesto?

I don't know if Dylan is truly describing himself—apparently he's got some kind of hardcore band and perhaps he wrote the above statement for its shock value. Still, is it possible to even come up with these ideas if he didn't experience the state of mind that they imply?

Fundamentally different

The truly scary thing about sociopaths is that they are fundamentally different from the rest of us. They do not want what we want. They do not value what we value.

Normal human beings want affection, cooperation and achievement. We want to care about others and contribute to life. Sociopaths want power, control and sex, and they'll destroy anyone and anything to get what they want.

But sociopaths look like us and appear to act like us. That's why they are so hard to identify. It's also why people who have not experienced their manipulation up close and personal find it so difficult to believe us. The uninitiated — those lucky souls who have not been devastated by a sociopath — have yet to learn that there are people in the world for whom proclamations of love, truth and promises are nothing but tactics in a power game.

Everything changes

This is the bottom line: Dealing with a sociopath changes everything. Normal human courtesies do not apply. Social protocols do not apply. Rules do not apply. Contracts do not apply. Laws do not apply.

If we find that we are interacting with a sociopath, the best thing we can do is get the person out of our lives. When that is not possible, we need to be on mental red alert at all times and understand that anything the person says may be a lie. We need to know that for the sociopath, we are not a friend, or a lover, or a relative, or a co-worker. For a sociopath, all we are is a target.

The flaw in viewing sociopaths through normal eyes

Lovefraud recently received an e-mail from a young man, we'll call him Kyle, who has just broken up with a woman whom he now believes is a sociopath. Based on the behavior he described, I'd say the guy is right. The woman cheated on him, and when confronted, either downplayed her behavior, said it was none of his business, or verbally attacked him. She had no interest in resolving problems. "Her solution to everything was to run, wait awhile, and then pile on affection as if nothing ever happened," Kyle wrote.

Kyle has been researching sociopathy to try to grasp what is really going on with this woman. Here's more of his email, which I have reproduced with his permission:

> First of all, I don't believe criminal behavior, monetary fraud, substance abuse, or any other overt signs of social misconduct are primary symptoms of sociopathy. I suppose that's the big question though... what is a primary sign? My theory is that the sociopath is incapable of developing personal values through the process of induction, meaning they are unable to look within themselves to gain a sense of self-esteem. This results their inability to experience empathy. After all, if one cannot generate a sense of self worth from their own reasoning how can they be expected to relate to others who do?
>
> It seems in every case I have read about, the sociopath is an extravert. I think this is natural as the person must constantly be in contact with others because they find no satisfaction in themselves. Sociopaths also seem to be universally intelligent. (Perhaps these are the factors that dif-

ferentiate a sociopath from a psychopath. Again, forgive my ignorance on the subject). What results is a charming individual who preys on other people to satisfy an endless hunger for temporary esteem. Because they cannot make sense of the internal values that should be generating this esteem, they simply try to get it from others, essentially reversing cause and effect.

In the end, this system never quite works, so they develop an incredible defense to avoid the fact that every close relationship falls apart. Every interaction is bounded by a series of rules/parameters. So long as the victim stays within these, things run smoothly. However, close human contact results in an emotional trade off that is impossible to control. Normally this is a tremendously good thing: trust, loyalty, and compassion are established. However, these all rely on a person's sense of self worth, and the sociopath is not able to understand that. Sooner or later the relationship becomes too close and loses all stability. This is the point where the sociopath is "found out."

In dealing with the woman, I felt a certain childlike quality to her emotions throughout our relationship. Though she was highly developed socially, in a lot of ways I almost felt like I was dealing with a puppy who just killed a small bird in the front yard. I think my mistake was in believing that I would be different. If I held my hand out she wouldn't bite it. But I think this quality is misleading, as that naiveté is something the sociopath will avoid at all costs. They simply refuse to learn from their mistakes, or even acknowledge them in the first place. It seems to be a rare combination of a highly developed intellect and a poorly developed emotional response.

Perhaps at some point every sociopath learns to guard that core of insecurity at the deepest level and as such cannot even look at that, let alone analyze it and learn from it. In time, they develop an incredibly complex mechanism to guard this, adding another component with each deception. By early adulthood, these deceptions become so many that the cost is just too great to turn back, and it's just so much easier to keep going that the thought never even crosses their mind.

These people are not normal

Kyle has correctly observed many traits of a sociopath: Criminality, fraud and substance abuse are not necessarily the prime indicators of this personality disorder. Sociopaths do not experience empathy. Sociopaths are extraverts. They are highly developed socially, but emotionally immature. They do not learn from mistakes.

However, his theories on why sociopaths are the way they are suffer from a fatal flaw: They are developed from the perspective of someone who is normal.

The hardest part of understanding what happened during our entanglements with sociopaths is coming to terms the extent to which these people are not normal.

Lovefraud readers have described sociopaths as not human. Aliens inhabiting human bodies. As cold as these descriptions may sound, they're probably the easiest way to grasp what you are dealing with in a relationship with a sociopath.

So how different are they? Let's take a look.

What sociopaths want

Normal people want love and harmonious relationships with others. Normal people want to feel competent in some form of endeavor. Normal people want to contribute to the world in some way.

Sociopaths want power, control and sex. Since they do not really value human relationships, they only want to win.

Kyle is correct in stating that sociopaths cannot look within themselves and develop personal values. He is incorrect in assuming that this causes the sociopath distress. Yes, these disordered people are empty inside, and they may be vaguely aware that they are missing something. But most sociopaths do not have issues with their self-esteem. If anything, they are grandiose, and their views of themselves are ridiculously inflated. They feel absolutely entitled to anything that they want, simply because they want it.

Self-esteem and sociopaths

Kyle speculates that sociopaths must be in constant contact with other people because they are trying to borrow self-esteem from others. This is not the case. Sociopaths view people as pawns to be manipulated into giving them what they want. Every social encounter is a potential feeding opportunity, a chance to convince someone to provide something.

Many people, of course, eventually catch on that they are being used, and stop serving as supply to the sociopaths. Sociopaths are aware of this—they've experienced it many times. So they are constantly on the lookout for new targets. When one victim is depleted, he or she must be replaced with another.

This leads to the answer to Kyle's question, which is, "what is a primary sign of sociopathy?" Dr. Leedom has said lying. Steve Becker has said exploitative behavior. Put them together and you can say deceitful exploitation is central to the disorder.

Insecurity and sociopaths

Kyle suggests that sociopaths are insecure and build defense mechanisms to protect themselves from being hurt. By the time they're adults, these defense mechanisms are so elaborate and complex that sociopaths can't return to their authentic selves.

Again, he's trying to interpret the sociopath based on how normal people may cope with personal issues. This is a mistake.

Wikipedia defines insecurity as, "a feeling of general unease or nervousness that may be triggered by perceiving oneself to be unloved, inadequate or worthless." Sociopaths probably should see themselves as unloved, inadequate or worthless, but they don't. They may seem to be exhibiting insecurity, but in reality it's one of two things:

- Frustration that they're not getting what they want.
- Manipulation tactics to get what they want.

Many sociopaths, particularly antisocials and psychopaths, have no feelings, so there are no feelings to hurt. They can certainly pretend to be hurt, but it is a ruse designed to guilt others

171

into giving them what they want.

Genetic roots

So if sociopaths are not trying to protect their deeply felt insecurities, where does this disorder come from? In most cases, the temperamental traits that lead to sociopathy are genetic. That usually means one of the parents is a sociopath, and sociopaths are notoriously bad parents. If children are born with the traits, bad parenting can make them develop the full disorder.

But even if a child with the traits gets good parenting, the disorder can develop. Parents who have a child at risk of developing sociopathy need to take extra steps to help the child overcome his or her predisposition, but the parents may not realize it. And in some cases, even the best parenting is not enough to overcome negative genetics.

Accept and avoid

Please understand that I am not picking on Kyle. He's obviously given a lot of thought to his experience with a sociopathic woman, and is trying to understand what happened. He has a reasonably good handle on normal behavior and normal motivations.

His letter provided me with an opportunity to illustrate that what we know and understand about normal human behavior simply does not apply to sociopaths. Thank you, Kyle, for allowing me to quote you.

In the end, we may not be able to truly comprehend sociopaths. The way they go through life is just too foreign to our natures. We must accept that they are very, very different from us, learn to recognize the symptoms, and if we see them, run for the hills.

Sociopaths and sex:
neither straight nor gay

Many women have written to Lovefraud about husbands who they've come to believe are sociopaths. They were astounded to discover that, not only was the husband cheating, but he was having sex with men.

Lovefraud reader eyeswideshut writes about this in a recent comment to the post, *After he's gone: looking at the sociopath through open eyes*. She asks:

> Now that I know he is also gay, is sociopathic tendency in married gay men not common as well? When I read the stories of the women in the book ("Straight Wives"), many of the men sound like sociopaths as well. Have you studied this phenomenon? Is it possible that gay men who choose to live the lie of married life are likely also socios?

To this, another Lovefraud reader, Leslie, commented:

> On the third extended date I had with the SP, I turned to him one night, after we'd been together, and said, "Have you been with men?" Something in the way he'd made love made me think he had. He stared at the window and said in a monotone, "I have never made love to a man." It was the same monotone he used to deny that he was living with a woman when I asked him that a year later. He was. I don't have hard proof, but I know the guy had had sex with men.

Then alohatraveler commented:

I have heard from another victim of my sociopath that he was starting to get more "experimental" when she knew him. She knew him after me. He was expressing an interest in having sex with a man, but of course, with a woman present, because he was "not gay." We both also saw an ad that he posted looking for sex with a transsexual. Then he placed an ad where he wanted a traditional type of woman.

"Not a gay bone in my body"

Shortly after I met my sociopathic ex-husband, James Montgomery, he proclaimed to me, "There's not a gay bone in my body." I had no reason to doubt him. But when I left him after two and a half years, I learned a lot about his sexual activities:

- He had sex with at least six other women during our relationship.
- He was heavily into Internet porn.
- He solicited gay male prostitutes.
- He tried to arrange threesomes and looked for swinging couples.

In short, he wanted sexual thrills. The more different kinds of thrills, the better. I'm lucky I didn't get a serious disease.

Screw anyone

Sociopaths are hard-wired for sex. They have an excessive need for stimulation, excitement and sensation. They also have no fear and no inhibitions. From a sexual perspective, that means a voracious appetite and anything goes.

So when it comes to sexual orientation, I believe sociopaths are neither straight nor gay. In short, they'll screw anyone.

Lovefraud has heard from gay individuals—men and women— who were involved in gay relationships with sociopaths. I asked several of them if they thought the sociopath was actually gay. They all agreed with my theory and said the sociopath was not gay.

Sex with an agenda

This does not mean, however, that sociopaths are out of control. On the contrary, to them, sex, and sexual orientation, is just something to be used in order to achieve their objective, whatever that is.

Perhaps the most egregious example of this is the case of James McGreevey, the former governor of New Jersey. McGreevey, you may recall, resigned from office after proclaiming in a news conference that he was a "gay American."

The truth was that his political career was imploding under a series of scandals. As I wrote in a review of the book written by McGreevey's wife, I believe the former governor played the gay card because it was the best way to spin his political collapse.

Sociopaths use people for sex, and use sex to get what they want. Anybody who suits their agenda will do.

If it suits their agenda to be married with children, then that's what they'll do. But if sociopaths indulge in same-sex relationships, in my opinion, it's because they're sociopaths, not gay.

Most cheaters are amateurs; sociopaths are professionals

Lovefraud recently received a very nice email from the editor of HowToDoThings.com, complimenting the information provided by Lovefraud. She suggested that an article from her website might be of interest to Lovefraud readers. It is called *How To Recognize the Signs of Cheating Men.*

I checked out the article. Now, I mean absolutely no disrespect to HowToDoThings.com, but the article describes cheating by mere amateurs, not sociopaths.

According to the article, all of the following should raise a woman's suspicions that her guy might be cheating:

1. He improves his personal appearance.
2. He finds fault with you.
3. Your sex life changes.
4. He uses a new phone or other new technologies.
5. Your intuition tells you something is wrong.
6. His routine changes, or he has new interests.
7. His work or financial habits change.
8. You find evidence of another woman.

The key here is that something about the guy's behavior is different. I'm sure this is the case if a guy who is reasonably normal, albeit bored or unhappy, strays. But it's not the case with sociopaths.

For sociopaths, cheating is a way of life, so there is no change to notice.

Cheating by professionals

Sociopaths — both men and women — are professional cheaters, liars and manipulators. So let's take a look at the list in the context of a sociopath.

1. There probably won't be a change in personal appearance. Either they're always obsessive about how they look, or they rely on their skills of seduction.
2. After initial flattery to get you hooked, a sociopath will start finding fault with you. In time, the sociopath blames you for being the source of all problems.
3. Sociopaths always have plenty of sexual tricks and incredible stamina, so they'll continue to get sex from you, even if they're getting it from someone else.
4. A new phone is simply another new toy, and sociopaths love toys. In fact, they'll get you to buy the toys.
5. Your intuition has probably always been telling you something is wrong. But sociopaths have so many glib explanations that you no longer trust your own perceptions.
6. Sociopaths are always coming and going, and they're always starting something new. After awhile, you accept this as normal.
7. A sociopath is always irresponsible. Jobs and money just disappear. This, too, becomes normal.
8. When you find direct evidence of cheating, the sociopath either explains it away, or accuses you of being paranoid.

The problem about being involved with a sociopath is that he or she is always erratic, and you are always off balance. So it's difficult to see the signs of cheating, especially as the sociopath continues to profess his or her love and concern for you.

In fact, you may never find out the extent of the cheating until the sociopath discards you. Only then, when the sociopath no longer bothers to spin a web of deceit, might you find out what was really going on.

What is a sociopath feeling?

Lovefraud recently received the following letter with an important question from a reader:

> "I am trying to understand what the sociopath is feeling. Do they feel love? Do they love? What hurts a sociopath? How can you communicate with a sociopath?"

The problem in dealing with a sociopath is that they are fundamentally different from the rest of us. The extent of their difference is truly difficult to comprehend — until you've had a close encounter with one of them.

Let's look at these questions individually. The answers are specific to sociopaths who have antisocial or narcissistic personality disorder, or psychopathy.

1. Do they feel love?

The short answer is no. In order to feel love, a person must be able to feel empathy. Sociopaths do not feel empathy for other people.

Those of us who are capable of empathy may feel joy when a friend or relative has a baby, or want to help disaster victims by sending a donation, or cry at a poignant TV commercial. A sociopath does not have an emotional reaction to any of these scenarios. Whether due to genetic make-up, or a traumatic upbringing, or both, when it comes to feeling emotional connections to other people, sociopaths simply don't get it.

They do, however, learn that by simulating an emotional reaction, or generating an emotional reaction in another person, they can get what they want. So they fake it. They mouth the words, "I love you." For good measure, they plead, "I don't want to lose you," with tears running down their cheeks.

It is all an act.

A sociopath may be telling you that he or she loves you. What the sociopath really means is that he or she wants you like a hot new Lexus. You can do something for the sociopath—such as provide transportation. You can make the sociopath look good—providing a status symbol or the appearance of normalcy. The only reason a sociopath may be upset if you and the kids leave is because he or she doesn't want to part with possessions.

2. What does a sociopath feel?

One of the key symptoms of a psychopath (a type of sociopath), is shallow emotion. In his book *Without Conscience*, Dr. Robert Hare writes,

> "Psychopaths seem to suffer a kind of emotional poverty that limits the range and depth of their feelings. While at time they appear cold and unemotional, they are prone to dramatic, shallow and short-lived displays of feeling."

They can feel anger and rage, but it typically doesn't last very long and has no depth. Many people are mystified by the way in which sociopaths can turn emotions on and off. For example, the Lovefraud reader who asked the questions in the beginning of this post also wrote about his ex-wife:

> "We met with a court mediator during our divorce proceedings. After accusing me of the most horrible things you can imagine, once away from the mediator, she broke down and cried hysterically asking, 'Why are you doing this to me?' Ten minutes later she was bubbly and acting for the judge."

One expert, Dr. J. Reid Maloy, wrote that psychopaths often feel "contemptuous delight" when they have successfully deceived someone. He also notes that they frequently feel boredom—which then prompts them to aggressively find stimulation, such as someone new to manipulate.

3. What hurts a sociopath?

Sociopaths do not experience hurt feelings as the rest of us do. They may pretend to be hurt in order to manipulate you, but again, it is an act.

This is an important concept for anyone trying to break free of a sociopath to understand. If you are breaking off a relationship, there is no reason to be nice. You do not have to try to let the sociopath down slowly or gently. Just say, "It's over," and leave. Then maintain a strict policy of No Contact.

You cannot hurt a sociopath's feelings. He or she doesn't have any.

4. How can you communicate with a sociopath?

Understand that a sociopath looks at every interaction with another person as an opportunity for manipulation. Therefore, your best policy with a sociopath is No Contact.

If you must communicate with a sociopath, always be on mental red alert. As Dr. Liane Leedom writes, the cardinal sign of sociopathy is lying. Anything said to you may be a lie, or, at best, a twisting of the truth. Furthermore, anything you say to the sociopath, any information you provide, may be used against you.

Here are some tips for communicating with a sociopath:

1. Provide as little information as possible.
2. Document everything. Get communications in writing. If you are communicating verbally, have a witness.
3. Do not trust. Verify.
4. Be explicit and lay down the law. If the sociopath violates any terms, there must be consequences.

Implications of no empathy and no fear

Antisocials, narcissists and psychopaths do not feel empathy.

As Dr. Liane Leedom and other experts have written, they also do not feel fear. Empathy and fear are the basic components of remorse and guilt—so they don't feel those emotions, either.

What does all this mean? These sociopaths do not really care about people. They do not feel obliged to comply with society's rules. They cannot be trusted to "do the right thing." They have no morals.

That — in all its emptiness — is their true nature.

Why sociopaths succeed:
Style matters more than substance

Charismatic, glib, grandiose, magnetic, energetic — sociopaths are typically described in these terms. No matter what they actually do and say, these men and women have style.

And, according to a classic experiment in education research, style is all that is needed to be respected and believed.

Back in 1970, Dr. Donald H. Naftulin, director of Continuing Education in Psychiatry at the University of Southern California School of Medicine, and colleagues, conducted an experiment to test the hypothesis that student ratings of educators depend largely on personality variables and not on educational content.

The experiment was ingenious, and in my opinion, the results go a long way towards explaining why sociopaths get away with portraying themselves as experts on topics about which they know absolutely nothing.

Research method

This was the experiment: Eleven psychiatrists, psychologists and social worker educators, who were attending an educational conference, were invited to a lecture on, "Mathematical Game Theory as Applied to Physician Education." The speaker was Dr. Myron L. Fox, who was introduced as an accomplished expert on game theory.

In reality, "Dr. Fox" was an actor hired to play the part of an expert, and he knew nothing at all about game theory.

Even worse, he was instructed to talk in circles. According to the scientific paper about the experiment, *The Doctor Fox Lecture: A Paradigm of Educational Seduction*, published by the Journal of Medical Education in 1973:

One of the authors, on two separate occasions, coached the lecturer to present his topic and conduct his question and answer period with an excessive use of double talk, neologisms, non sequiturs, and contradictory statements. All this was to be interspersed with parenthetical humor and meaningless references to unrelated topics.

That's exactly what the actor did. "Dr. Fox" began his lecture with:

It was not long before they realized that game theory was not primarily concerned with disclosing the optimum strategy, what it really is concentrating on is concerned with the logic of conflict, that is, with the theory of strategy.

Now, in this way, interestingly enough, here in the gambling state of Nevada, the question could be asked, "Does game theory differ from gambler's choice?" where there is a conflict of interest between the two parties, out of which one is to emerge victorious and one is to be defeated.

It sounds good, but on closer inspection, "Dr. Fox" said absolutely nothing. The actor kept it up for an hour, and then took questions for a half-hour. Throughout his entire presentation, he didn't say anything that made sense, but no one in the audience of professional educators figured out that the lecture was a sham.

In fact, they loved him. An eight-question evaluation after the presentation was overwhelmingly positive. One person commented,

Excellent presentation, enjoyed listening. Has warm manner. Good flow, seems enthusiastic. What about the two types of games, zero-sum and non-zero sum? Too intellectual a presentation. My orientation is more pragmatic.

Educational seduction

Dr. Fox's presentation was videotaped and shown to two more groups. The second group was 11 more psychiatrists, psychologists and psychiatric social workers, who were all identified as mental health educators. The third group comprised 33 educators and administrators enrolled in a graduate level university educational philosophy course.

The results: When the second two groups filled out their evaluations, they, too, were overwhelmingly positive about Dr. Fox.

The authors of the study described the results as "educational seduction." They wrote:

> The notion that students, even if they are professional educators, can be effectively "seduced" into an illusion of having learned if the lecturer simulates a style of authority and wit is certainly not new. In a terse but appropriate statement on educators, Postman and Weingartner emphasized that "it is the sign of a competent crap detector that he is not completely captivated by the arbitrary abstractions of the community in which he happened to grow up." The three groups of learners in this study, all of whom had grown up in the academic community and were experienced educators, obviously failed as "competent crap detectors" and were seduced by the style of Dr. Fox's presentation. Considering the educational sophistication of the subjects, it is striking that none of them detected the lecture for what it was.

This phenomenon of "educational seduction," that a student's perception of learning was significantly affected by the instructor's presentation style, not the content of the lecture, is called the "Dr. Fox effect."

Repeatedly replicated

According to an article published last year on PsychologyToday.com called *The Return of Dr. Fox*, the original study has been repeatedly replicated. A recent version concluded that students were aware that they didn't actually learn anything, even though they continued to rate the speaker highly.

A controversial conclusion of this research was that student evaluations of teachers couldn't be trusted. Other people argue that educational seduction does not exist.

To me, the more important point is that people, including professional mental health educators, are likely to regard a person and his or her message positively based solely on style. Someone who speaks with authority, energy and warmth will be respected and believed, even if the content of the communication is total nonsense.

Unfortunately, the human tendency to respond to style over substance plays right into the hands of sociopaths. All they have to do is speak with confidence and turn on the charm, and we believe them. It's a human failing that makes us all susceptible to deception and manipulation.

10 reasons why psychopaths get away with it

Why is it that psychopaths frequently get away with cheating, abuse, backstabbing, fraud, theft, and other nefarious activities — even murder? Here are 10 strategies that these exploiters may employ to escape accountability.

1. Psychopaths lie fluently and convincingly

They lie while looking you right in they eye, without a trace of nervousness or guilt. If they're caught in a lie, they easily lie to cover the lie. It's no wonder they are believed.

2. Psychopaths protest with righteous indignation

They say they would NEVER do such a thing, and HOW can you possibly accuse THEM of such behavior? Everyone doubts you, and you even doubt yourself.

3. Psychopaths smear their accuser/target

If that's you, they ruin your credibility, often starting the smear campaign long before you even realize what they've done to you. When everything blows up, you have no support.

4. Psychopaths become whatever will serve their agenda

Should they express remorse? Pull rank? Plead ignorance? Portray the bumbling fool? They'll do whatever enables them to escape consequences.

5. Psychopaths plan many moves in advance

They plot and scheme, lining up allies, fall guys, minions, bank accounts, transfers, even replacement romantic partners. Then

186

they make their move.

6. Psychopaths grab targets of opportunity

They are always on the lookout for someone who is useful to their agenda. If you have something they want, they figure out where you are vulnerable and use it against you.

7. Psychopaths know how to go right up to the line without crossing it

Psychopaths often engage in behavior that is immoral and unethical, but not illegal. Or, the situations are he said/she said, with no proof of anything. There is nothing to prosecute.

8. Psychopaths size up and flatter whomever they need to convince

Is it a boss, a police officer, a therapist, a judge? They align themselves with that person, pretend to be on the same team, and turn an adversary into an ally.

9. Psychopaths have the dirt on whoever is passing judgment

They put adversaries, work superiors and legal authorities in compromising positions, and then engage in blackmail. Suddenly, the case is dropped.

10. Psychopaths expect to get away with their actions

They believe they can talk themselves out of anything, or divert attention to someone else. In many cases, they've been doing it successfully all their lives.

Okay, sometimes psychopaths have to face the consequences of their actions. After all, experts say 25 percent of the prison population are psychopaths. But even those who are locked up probably got away with a lot of bad behavior before they were finally put behind bars.

Never underestimate a psychopath.

Why sociopaths cheat

Lovefraud received an email from a reader whom we'll call "Ingrid." She brought up a question that I've heard over and over:

> Just wondering if you could tell me why sometimes they stay with others longer as I feel he wants this new woman for his main supply even though he was trying for a baby with me, what does a main supply have that I didn't? He seems settled with her.

Ingrid, most sociopaths cheat on their romantic partners. In fact, they are often cheating throughout the entire relationship, but it may take you a while to find out about it. Or you may have caught hints that the sociopaths were cheating, but they were able to explain the situations away. Eventually, however, you have so much evidence that you can no longer ignore their infidelity, even if they keep lying about it.

Admitting the truth to yourself, you are hurt and angry at their betrayal. You may also feel that in some way you were not "good enough," and that's why the sociopath strayed. The sociopath may actually tell you that — but don't believe it.

What you need to understand is that sociopaths will cheat regardless of who you are or what you do.

Here is the basic truth: Sociopaths engage in romantic relationships not for love, but for exploitation. If a sociopath engages in a romantic relationship, it's because the romantic partner is a target who has something that the sociopath wants.

So what does the sociopath want? It could be anything. Here are some possibilities:

1. Sex. Even if you are having regular, rambunctious sex with the sociopath, he or she will always be looking for a new sexual adventure. The new target may not be younger or more attractive — it's just someone different.

2. Money. Many sociopaths are always on the lookout for someone whom they can scam for money. This is especially true if you are running low on funds because the sociopath has already convinced you to spend all your cash and run up your credit cards.

3. Housing. Sociopaths may like the new target's accommodations better than yours. Or, the sociopaths may suspect that you're getting ready to kick them to the curb, so they need a backup plan for living arrangements.

4. Connections. Sociopaths are frequently cooking up some "deal" or "project" — code for a scam — and the new target may know someone who knows someone who could be talked into participating.

5. Entertainment. Sociopaths sometimes start romantic pursuits for the fun of it, just to see if they can catch the target. This often happens with online involvements. Sociopaths keep sending texts and emails, proclaim love, promise to get together — and never show up. They never planned to show up — the whole involvement is nothing but a game.

These are just a few of the possible reasons sociopaths cheat. The truth is sociopaths do not even need a reason. The cheating may simply be that an opportunity presents itself and the sociopath pounces.

Sociopaths are incapable of love

If your romantic partner exhibits most or all of the key symptoms of a sociopath, and you discover cheating, please don't ask yourself, "What does that person have that I don't have?"

Despite what sociopaths said in the past, they don't love you and they never did, because they are incapable of love. So a new target just means that the sociopath has found someone else to exploit.

No happily ever after

So Ingrid, please understand:

1. There is no point in being a sociopath's "main sup-ply." The main supply is just someone who has more to lose to the sociopath.
2. Perhaps the new target does have something that you didn't have. Again, it means she has something else that the sociopath wants to take. This is not good for her.
3. If the sociopath seems "settled," it's only because the sociopath is engaged in a full-court press to snag the new target. Once she has been drained of every-thing the sociopath wants, she, too, will be dis-carded.

When sociopaths move on to new targets, you may want to feel sorry for them, but not jealous. No one lives happily ever after with a sociopath. All involvements are bad; it's just a matter of how much damage the sociopath inflicts.

Letter to Lovefraud:
Is his goal to break me?

Editor's Note: This Letter to Lovefraud is from a reader whom we'll call "Aubree." Names have been changed.

I recently got out of a two-year relationship with a person who I believe is a sociopath, or at the very least an extremely vengeful borderline. When we first got together, he told me that he used to have a habit of going to bars, finding the prettiest and most confident-looking woman there, and proceeding to go up to her and start picking on her and making fun of her for something that he suspected she might be insecure about. For example, if he saw a girl who was beautiful but wasn't stick-thin, he'd go up to her and start making snide remarks about her weight. He said he enjoyed doing this because he got pleasure out of "knocking these women down off their high horse."

Of course, it shocked me that he would do something like that, but he brushed it off and swore it was in the past, saying that he wouldn't dream of doing it again. He was also a huge jokester — typical life-of-the-party type of personality — and some part of me wanted to believe he was just telling me stories, exaggerating. Looking back, however, I should have heeded that red flag. Over time, he started to take little shots and digs at me, designed to put me down or make me feel unsure of myself. He went from worshiping the ground I walked on to cutting me down. Every time he did this, I called him out on it, and he said he respected that because I "didn't take his crap." But every now and then, there was another backhanded remark coming my way. I often got the sense that he secretly

HATED me. Sometimes I'd wake up in the morning and he'd be in bed next to me, just STARING at me. But it wasn't a loving, warm, doting stare. It was an icy, CREEPY stare. It's like there were daggers flying out of his eyes and straight at me.

In addition, every time something good happened to me — like my choosing to go back to school or getting a new car — I would always sense this underlying contempt and rage coming from him, like a seething resentment. I knew in my gut that he didn't want me to be happy or to thrive — even though he would swear up and down that my happiness and success were TOP priority to him — but I couldn't wrap my head around why he would be so malicious and hateful towards me. I didn't want it to make sense.

There is much, much more that went on in this relationship — typical idealize/devalue/discard, complete with love-bombing, I could write much more — but I wanted to write you because I'm wondering if my sociopath's motivation for getting into a relationship with me was purely to destroy me as a person, to "knock me off my high horse" like he tried to do to those other women? He never took any money from me or anything like that, and never used me for anything physical (I was more into sex than he was). All he ever said to me in the beginning of our relationship was that I "had a light about me" and that I had a happiness that he didn't have. I'm wondering if it was for this reason that he targeted me, so that he could whittle away my confidence, shame me and eventually break me down? In other words, so that he could "win" by stripping me of what made me, me? It seems so foolish to me that someone would want to steal another person's happiness or positive traits or destroy their confidence, but I can't think of any other motivation in his case. He always had to be the center of attention and was constantly complaining that I was the "better looking of the two of us" and the "smarter one" (he had never gone to school and was working an aimless job not fit for a man his age). It's like he didn't want the spotlight to be on me, ever. He really seemed like a bona fide misogynist to me.

I know you have a wealth of information on sociopaths and you've read so many first-hand accounts, so I'd love to hear any thoughts or insight you have on my situation. Thanks,
"Aubree"

Donna Andersen responds

Aubree,

Yes, it is certainly possible that this man's only motivation was exactly as you stated — to destroy you.

Sociopaths engage in romantic relationships for exploitation. Usually, they exert power and control in order to obtain money, sex, a place to live, domestic services, or some other obvious advantage.

But with some sociopaths, the exploitation takes a more sinister form. They exert power and control simply to entertain themselves. They enjoy the idea of being a puppet master. They manipulate you for the fun of it.

You may remember the movie *Dangerous Liaisons,* starring Glenn Close, John Malkovich and Michelle Pfeiffer. In this story, seduction was a game, with the objective of ruining people's reputations and breaking their hearts.

Well, some sociopaths engage in this game. People have told me how they were pursued and pursued, and when they finally fell in love, the sociopath simply dumped them.

In other cases, breaking off a relationship isn't enough for a sociopath. He or she also wants to grind the former partner into the dirt.

It's truly difficult to comprehend just how heartless these people can be. All we can really do is accept that there are people for whom relationships are nothing but a sick game, and learn to recognize and avoid them.

The sociopathic MO
in three easy steps

I have a friend who lost his wife to cancer. After a year, he started going out in search of companionship. He knew my history of being involved with a sociopath, in fact, he knew my ex, James Montgomery. So when he had a bizarre experience with a woman he dated for a few weeks, my friend had questions for me.

The woman claimed to be separated from her husband, although I'm not sure that was the case. She pursued my friend relentlessly, until they had sex. At some point, she made a comment about "a lion needs fresh meat." After that, they spent an entire day together, then she unceremoniously dumped him.

My friend asked, was this woman kooky like my ex?

He told me more, and it sounded like the woman had sociopathic traits, although perhaps not the full-blown disorder. So we've been discussing this personality type. One conversation went like this:

My friend: "What's the first thing sociopaths do when they meet you?"

Me: "Evaluate you to see if you have something they want."

My friend: "What's the second thing they do?"

Me: "Look for your vulnerabilities."

My friend: "Then what?"

Me: "Then they figure out how to use your vulnerabilities to manipulate you.

Sociopathic MO

This short conversation identified the sociopathic MO, or modus operandi. Here it is:

- First, do you have something he or she wants?
- Second, what are your vulnerabilities?

- Third, how can they manipulate your vulnerabilities to get what they want?

Here is the brutal truth: Sociopaths view the world as predators and prey—they are the predators, everyone else is prey.

Feeding opportunities

Here's another brutal truth: Sociopaths view all social interactions as feeding opportunities.

So what do they want from their targets? In many cases, the answer is obvious—sex, money, a place to live, someone to support them.

But we also have to remember that sometimes, sociopaths just want entertainment. They want the fun of manipulating someone into doing what they want. They get a rush from getting over on their targets. These cons feed their primal desires that I've written about before—the desires for power and control.

My friend was shaking his head over the encounter with the predator female. Like all of us, he was having a hard time coming to grips with how soulless these people truly are.

With sociopaths,
words and actions can both be lies

Lovefraud received the following observation from a reader who posts as "new_day":

> I just had an A-ha moment while scrolling through Facebook. I read a post that said, "Words may lie but actions always tell the truth." The problem with understanding how sociopathic behavior is so damaging to others, is that we have to realize even Actions can Lie!!
>
> Those who are hollow of any truth or love are masters of acting! They can entertain us into thinking they are the good and loving soul mate that we were blessed to meet. In reality, it was all love fraud.
>
> Somehow, I am expected to move forward with the inability to trust another person's actions again.

This is a very astute observation. Anyone who has tangled with a sociopath knows that they lie. They tell big lies, small lies, outrageous lies and stupid lies. Sociopaths lie while looking deep into your eyes and clasping your hand in theirs, promising that they will never lie to you.

Unfortunately, humans are lousy lie detectors, especially in the beginning of a romantic involvement, as the liar is showering you with affection. When the sweet words include, "I'll love you forever," and "You're the one I've been waiting for all my life," well, who doesn't want to believe them?

Words and actions

The standard advice regarding sociopaths is to ignore their words and pay attention to their actions. But as this reader, new_day, points out, sometimes you can't pay attention to their actions either.

The actions of a sociopath may lie as well. They may take you out for a romantic dinner, play with your kids, help you take care of your house, buy flowers for your mother.

Usually, when someone engages in behaviors like these it's because they want to show that they care about you. When sociopaths take what seem to be caring, thoughtful actions, they have an agenda. They are behaving in a socially appropriate way because they are reeling you in for future exploitation, or creating an image that will benefit them in other exploitation projects.

Of course, you know this now, most likely after learning the hard way. So what does all this mean for your recovery? How do you move forward in life, and build new relationships, when you feel like you can't trust people's words and you can't trust people's actions.

You learn to trust yourself.

And how do you do that? By focusing on your own healing.

Trusting your internal signals

If you're like most people who became involved with sociopaths, you knew in your gut, from early in the involvement, that something was wrong. The story didn't add up; you had a bad feeling; you sensed something was amiss. But you didn't listen to yourself.

The biggest reason why you didn't trust your instincts was probably because you didn't know that sociopaths existed. You didn't know that people live among us who look just like us, but have no heart, no conscience and no remorse.

Now you know. You have the empirical knowledge to make sense of those internal warnings, if you ever feel them again.

But when you have a general mistrust of everyone, how do you differentiate between legitimate internal warnings and imagined internal warnings?

Value in healing

That's where the healing comes in. With healing, you become

comfortable with the concept that while most people are basically good, a certain segment of the population is not.

With healing, you learn to value yourself. You come to understand that you're the one who knows what is best for you. You feel comfortable walking away from anyone or anything that doesn't feel right, without waiting for objective proof that the situation is bad.

Now, even a good, solid recovery may not totally prevent sociopaths from coming into your life. There are simply too many of them among us, they're everywhere, and they're very, very good at their acts. So they may fool you for a while.

But with recovery, they won't fool you for long. And when your instincts start emitting warnings, you'll know what they mean.

Here's how I define success in spotting sociopaths: It's not keeping them out of your life entirely. It's getting them out of your life before they do serious damage.

When you learn to trust yourself, you can achieve that success.

Sociopaths change
our beliefs about being human

Lovefraud received the following email from a reader whom we'll call "Iris." She was married for 20 years to a man who she now realizes is a sociopath.

I avoid talking to my ex-husband as much as possible, but he is 4 months behind on court ordered spousal support as I am in school getting my business degree and working. He has to pay $600 a month for 3 years. The court also ordered the support to pay me back for $11,000 I had to put into our house and property to make it "sellable" after he left me in the dust and moved to another state. He left me with 5 acres, a house falling apart, a barn with code violations, and our 3 family dogs. I went into survival mode and got it all fixed and sold and re-homed all of my dogs (who I love and miss very much) through a wonderful adoption agency. He also owes me for a mortgage reimbursement check he forged my signature on and cashed after he talked the mortgage co. into sending it to him in Calif. I filed a police report.

I was hoping you could help me. I e-mailed him with the threat of taking him to court and he called several times before I answered. I try to avoid talking to him because I always feel I am being manipulated. Within our conversation, he was mean, evil, nice, ugly and caring and the same old guy. I brought up that I know how he operates and that it took distance for a lengthy period of time to see that he was a sociopath and smooth talker and that his agenda is to "win" and manipulate. I said many other things also. HE ADMITTED THAT HE OPERATES

DIFFERENTLY AND DOESNT FEEL THE SAME AS OTHERS. I was blown away. The only other time that he ever came close to this was when I was about to leave him several years ago when I found out he was cheating on me again. His exact words were, "I can't help it; I've always gotten a RUSH out of getting away with stuff. It's been like that since I was a kid."

I guess what I "need" to know is, why did that hit me so hard? Why did it make me so emotional when he said he operates differently? Why did it make me feel sorry for him? Why do I feel so exhausted and why can't I stop crying now? Does his admission make it that much more real? Did the reality that he really is a sociopath and my whole marriage was meaningless overwhelm me? I have been divorced for a year and a half and apart from him since Nov. 2008. We have a 21-year-old son. We have not even had to communicate much.

All I know is, I am still affected in a very dark way because of being with him for so long. I've been to a psychologist once a week for quite a while. It helps, but she doesn't KNOW what it actually feels like. Do you have any words of wisdom to help me move on? I am ok most of the time, but I don't trust anyone and can't even think about dating. I feel paralyzed sometimes and felt that way throughout my long marriage. I still find myself resorting back to thinking, "maybe it was me." Am I damaged for life? I am usually pretty busy, but when I have time on my hands, things still get dark and I am tired of feeling like this.

Extreme difference

One of the hardest things to wrap our brains around is the extreme degree to which sociopaths are different from us.

Sociopaths, especially antisocials, narcissists and psychopaths, have no heart, no conscience and no remorse. Think about what that means. Sociopaths are missing all the qualities that make up the core of our humanity.

This is why coming to terms with the idea that sociopaths exist is so difficult. In order to grasp the concept of sociopaths, we have to give up some of our most cherished beliefs about what it means to be a human being living in our society.

Exploding myths

In our society, we may have differing points of views as old or young, men or women, liberals or conservatives, religious or secular, management or labor, or any other polarity. Still, some cultural ideas are so widespread, and so entrenched, that they are regarded as axioms.

When sociopaths are factored in, however, these axioms are nothing but exploding myths. Here are a few:

1. We all want to be loved

Sociopaths don't care about love. They don't even feel love. They certainly do not feel empathy for fellow human beings. When they appear to be acting out of love, it is probably nothing but manipulation, a tactic to advance their agenda. Sociopaths only want three things: power, control and sex.

2. There's good in everyone

This, unfortunately, is not true. There are people in the world who are rotten to the core, and they're the sociopaths. But unaware of the inherent evil of these predators, we believe that everyone deserves a chance, a second chance, and even more chances. Sociopaths milk this belief by promising to reform, but they never do.

3. Parents love their children

Most of us probably believe that, even if our childhoods were imperfect, our parents loved us and did the best they could. We don't want to consider the idea that some parents simply don't care about their kids. But if sociopaths have any concern about their children, it's roughly equivalent to the concern they feel for an inanimate possession, like a flat screen TV. There is no real love.

4. Truth and justice will prevail

Many of us end up in legal battles with sociopaths, such as filing for divorce or claiming fraud. We approach the legal system assuming that we'll get a fair hearing and justice will be served. But for sociopaths, court is show time. They lie to suit their agendas, and judges either don't see it, or don't care. Court isn't about truth, it's about winning, and sociopaths are wired to win.

5. We should live according to the Golden Rule

"Do to others what you would like them to do to you." This rule of ethics is at the center of every major religious tradition. But if the "others" are sociopaths, living by the Golden Rule sets us up to be exploited. Treating them as we want to be treated, we'll eventually find ourselves drained, and the sociopaths on to new sources of supply.

Recovery

So how do we deal with the loss of what we thought were unshakeable truths? I think recovery has three aspects to it.

1. We accept that they are what they are

It is extremely unlikely that any sociopath, by the time he or she is an adult, is going to change. We must give up feeling guilty, or responsible, or even concerned. We may need to release grief or anger over what happened to us, but we must realize that there is nothing we can do about them.

2. We are grateful that we are not them

Although sociopaths probably don't realize it, theirs is an empty, barren existence. They do not feel love, they do not feel human connection, they do not feel the warmth of belonging to anything. We may be in pain, and temporarily feel paralyzed, but we can recover our humanity. They don't have a chance.

3. We resolve never to be exploited again

Now we know that sociopaths exist. We know how they think. We know how they act. We will never lose this knowledge, and knowledge is power. We take back our power, establish our boundaries and move forward.

Yes, the experience of a sociopath rattles us to the core. But it is possible to learn from it, gather ourselves and live again, with much more wisdom than we had before the nasty encounter.

About the author

Donna Andersen is author of Lovefraud.com, a website that teaches people to recognize and recover from sociopaths. She is also author of *Red Flags of Love Fraud—10 signs you're dating a sociopath* and the *Red Flags of Love Fraud Workbook.*

Donna learned about sociopaths the hard way—by marrying one. She tells the whole outrageous story in her first book, *Love Fraud—How marriage to a sociopath fulfilled my spiritual plan.* The book was awarded five stars by the Midwest Book Review.

Donna founded Lovefraud Education and Recovery. The non-profit offers online webinars to help professionals and the public spot, escape and recover from narcissists, antisocials, psychopaths and other manipulators. She is co-author of a scientific paper about therapy for victims of sociopaths, and has presented research to the Society for the Scientific Study of Psychopathy.

Donna has appeared on television shows including *Insight* in Australia, *ABC News 20/20, Who the Bleep Did I Marry?, My Life is a Lifetime Movie, Handsome Devils* and *The Ricki Lake Show.* She has been interviewed for multiple radio shows, print articles and web posts.

Donna graduated summa cum laude from the Syracuse University with degrees in magazine journalism and psychology. She was the original editor of Atlantic City Magazine, and then founded a boutique advertising agency, Donna Andersen Copywriting, in 1983. Her portfolio includes multimedia scriptwriting, freelance magazine articles, newsletters, web content and more.

Donna is happily remarried, proving that recovery from betrayal is possible.